2012/2013 Tax Year

Contents

1

Introducing
The Larder, The Fridge & The Freezer.

No matter what age you are, whether you have a lump sum or are looking to save to build one up; whether you are retired already or are saving for retirement; the first step to understanding your money is breaking it down into three main categories:

Short term

Medium term

Long term

Anyone who has ever been to an adviser will have been told this already because they want you to invest in the long term products that make them money. In fact it is quite hard to get advice on short and medium term aspects of your finances because no one other than banks makes any money out of these areas. Due to recent FSA (Financial Services Authority) regulations the banks themselves are no longer allowed to advise you on banking (short term) and saving (medium term) products – they can only tell you about what is available and let you make your own decisions.

An analogy that is often used to help people understand the concept of short, medium and long term finances is that of the larder, fridge and freezer.

The larder represents your **current account**

The fridge represents your **medium term cash savings**

The freezer represents your **longer term investments**

Despite this being a well used and popular analogy, many still find it hard to grasp how all this works together as a strategy for your finances. This book will explore and expand on the analogy to help make this basic concept of money more understandable.

To begin with, imagine that the money you earn is like your vegetable patch. During harvest time for each vegetable you grow you have an abundance of that veg, let's say for example, green beans.

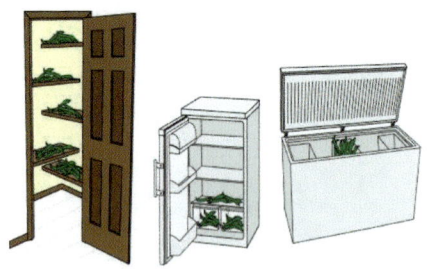

To effectively manage your harvest and not have any waste, you would put some fresh green beans in to your larder to use within the next couple of days. Some will be put in to the fridge for use within the next week. The rest you would put in to your freezer so that you have it to use in the winter when there is no fresh veg at all. Albeit on a timescale of a lifetime and with cash instead of green beans, this is the same concept for your finances.

In your harvesting years (income earning years up to retirement) you put the majority of money into your larder (current account) for immediate use. Any surplus goes into your fridge (savings accounts) for use in the near future. A small amount should also be put into your freezer (longer term savings) for use in the distant future. The idea is that over time, what is in your freezer builds up so that you can use it to survive on when there is no harvest (retirement).

Where a lot of people go wrong with their finances is not putting anything (or not enough) into their freezer to stock up for the winter of their life. Just as winter is the most expensive time of the year, retirement is the most expensive time of your life. You're home a lot of the time so utility and food bills are higher, you have to entertain yourself so costs of hobbies and socialising increase and whilst all this is happening not only will the cost of living be increasing but you no longer have a regular income stream. Managing your finances in both your fridge and freezer effectively can ensure that you have a well stocked and comfortable winter!

Working years

Retirement Years

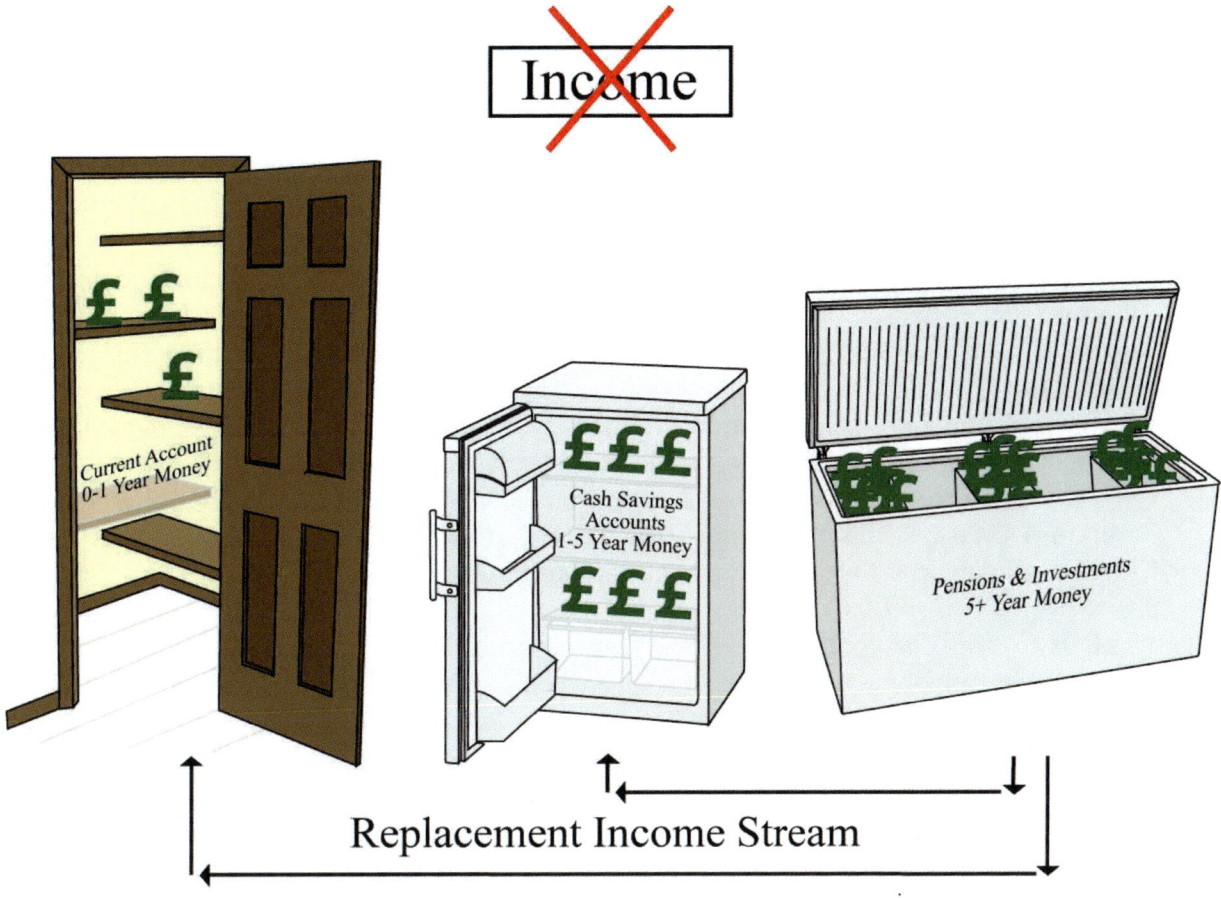

The rest of this book will explain how strategies for both your fridge and freezer can work and will help you understand the different products and choices you have for each one.

However, before you can start filling your fridge and freezer, you have to make sure your larder is in good order. Are you able to keep it filled for your everyday needs? (Or are you running out of money?)

2

Managing your larder

How many current accounts to have?

At a basic level you really need to have at least two – a larder and a cold cupboard.

Let me explain, you need one main current account that your income can go into and your direct debits, standing orders and bills can be paid out of – this is your larder. (A direct debit is a monthly payment that can fluctuate – for example a utility bill where your usage can change; a standing order is a set amount, such as your council tax.) Your cold cupboard should be an additional account that you can use for everyday spending including internet and phone purchases. Be sure to make it an account that you can easily transfer the funds into from your larder (i.e. by phone or online banking) or if you have a rough idea of how much you spend on purchases each month, you could set up a standing order to go into this account.

This is to limit the chance of having your account defrauded. If someone was to get hold of your personal details (most likely when using them over the phone or internet and with everyday usage) wouldn't you prefer that they did not have access to your main account with all your hard earned cash in it? Much better to only lose a tiny bit from a separate account! It is best to have a small overdraft on this second account so that if you spend a little more than usual you will have it covered without receiving any charges.

If you are trying to manage your everyday spending so that you do not go overdrawn on your main account and have bills bounce back unpaid, then a good idea is to work out exactly what you can spend each month and have this amount set up as a standing order from your larder (main account) into your cold cupboard (spending account). This way you know that your bills are always paid and exactly how much you have to spend each month. Avoiding those frustrating occasions when you think you have more than you do because one of your direct debits has come out later than usual and any extra spending pushes you into your overdraft.

If you are in control of your finances then you could consider using a credit card as your cold cupboard. By doing this you will have the added security of knowing that all of your purchases are insured but most credit cards also offer very good fraud protection services too. However, you must only do this if you are more than capable of paying off your spending each month so that you do not incur interest or charges. Do not use this as a way to live beyond your means.

If you are going to use a credit card as your cold cupboard/spending account, never take cash out on it. Only use it to make purchases, as the charges are phenomenal for cash withdrawals. Also avoid using the cheques they send you in the post as these are much the same as cash withdrawals when it comes to the interest you have to repay.

If you take out repayment cover insurance for your credit card, keep a track of what you spend during the month so you can pay it off before the bill arrives. Most cards charge an insurance fee per pound on what has been spent but if you pay the outstanding balance before the statement is produced, no fee will be incurred. By doing this you get the cover you need for any emergencies that may happen without paying for the cover when you don't need it.

If you are going to use a credit card for all purchases in this manner get one which offers 0% interest on purchases (you may need to change cards annually to take advantage of this). Also look into what spending benefits there are with the card. (i.e. do you get your spend amount rewarded with air miles, nectar points or similar?). Try to get as much benefit from the card as possible.

The benefits of benefit accounts

As mentioned earlier, getting advice on which account to use for your larder can be very difficult and in this day and age we are bombarded with different types of accounts and charges and it can be a minefield! Your choice needs to be a personal one with an account that suits your specific needs but here are some things to consider.

Benefit accounts. You know the ones…. pay so much a month and get all this for free! Nothing in life is free – particularly if it is an offer from a bank. I will say this now and doubtless say it again, the bank is NOT your friend, it is a business. It is there solely to make money from your money for shareholder profit. Few people grasp this and believe all the sales spin they are told when a bank is trying to befriend them for their cash.

OK, so back to benefit accounts. Firstly if you are going to have one of these accounts, don't be loyal to the bank that you are currently with, shop around. Make a list of what benefits each account gives and how much it costs each month. For example, they all offer free travel insurance but you need to check, does it cover your age group? Or does it cover the type of holiday you like to go on? Each account offers quite different coverage so you cannot assume it will give you the cover you require. If you're not careful, extra cover at the time of your holiday may end up costing you more than if you had a free bank account and bought your insurance somewhere else.

This is also the same for car breakdown services. Some of the benefit accounts have coverage from your door; some you need to be a ¼ of a mile from your home. When you break down at home and find the upgrade to the home start package costs more than a year's worth of cover with an alternative provider, you have to question if it has been worth the monthly cost of the account.

If you are considering one of these accounts make a list of the things you currently pay for monthly so you can identify where you may be able to make some savings. i.e. phone insurance, home emergency cover, breakdown cover etc. Write down how much you pay for each of these at the moment and what the cover is. Determine if you would be making a saving by switching to a paid account where you get the services for 'free'.

Finally the most important thing to do when you have one of these benefit accounts is **use it!** Make sure you take advantage of the free services you are provided with. Did you ever get around to registering your phone with the bank account insurance? This is how the banks make their profit. They know there will be a high percentage of customers who will forget they are paying a monthly fee for services they are not using.

Reward accounts

A new and popular type of benefit account is one that pays you each month for having a set amount of money going in. This can be worth doing and over the year could well save that little bit extra for Christmas or any other treat.

If you are in control of your finances enough to manage this kind of strategy then you could set up standing orders to go into the account, hit it with the funds it needs to give you the reward and then bounce back out again and back to your larder! For this to work you will need to ensure that you can live without the money each month for the length of time it takes for it to work its way through the system and back again (can be up to a week). If you have a partner then you can probably open up a joint account and two individual accounts, getting three lots of benefits!

How much to hold in your current account?

Those who don't grasp the concept of larder, fridge and freezer often use spare current accounts to save money in. This is not a good idea for many reasons: (1) you are not going to get much, if any, return on it; (2) it is too easy to dip into and spend; and (3) current accounts are the easiest accounts to defraud so you could potentially lose the lot.

Many leave large lump sums in their current account, like £10,000 or more, as a 'working balance'. This is a ludicrous idea for reasons (1) and (3) above. Why keep that level of funding in your current account if you do not use that much every month? If your answer to this is that you have a high interest current account then you must check the details of the account. Most high interest current accounts have an upper limit on what they will give you a good return on. Check this out, know how much it is and don't go above that limit. There is no point having £10,000 in a high interest current account if you are only getting a good return on the first £2,000. The chances are the rest of it will not only be losing value with inflation (more on this later) but also be at risk of being stolen.

Realistically, all you need in your current account is your monthly outgoings plus a little extra as a buffer for any unseen expenditure. If you want a contingency fund – which you should have (I will go into more details of these when looking at your fridge), then it should be in a different account and not kept in your current account.

Switching accounts

Loyalty is an age thing. The younger generation often have very little loyalty to any one provider and will jump ship at the drop of a hat. The older generation however, seems to be fiercely and often unjustifiably loyal to one provider.

Many people have their current account with one bank but will shop around with their savings. You should shop around with your current account too – get the best deal that suits you. In this day and age whether you are working or not you should be making sure that every single penny earns you as much as it possibly can. If this means changing your bank account then you should, but only after researching all that is on the market – don't just go with the bank that has the best salesperson.

If you are considering switching providers to obtain certain benefits then be absolutely sure how long those benefits are going to be offered for, before you switch. If there is no guarantee that you will receive the benefit for at least the next year (and in fact it could be stopped within a month of you moving over), question if you want to do this or not. You need to see these offers as they actually are – a hook to reel you in!

Although most banks offer hassle-free switching services, be cautious before changing all your direct debits and credits over. A good idea would be to open an account with the new bank to trial them out before you switch everything to them.

A summary of your larder

- It is best to have at least two separate current accounts, a main account for your credits and debits and a spending account. This will not only help you manage your finances but will also reduce the chance of having your main account defrauded.

- If you are going to have one of the new benefit accounts, make sure it gives you all the cover you need and take full advantage of the 'free' services provided.

- Don't use current accounts to save money in and don't keep high balances in there. You should only have your working balance plus a small buffer.

- Remember that banking staff are sales people and are targeted on most things the bank offers (such as current accounts with a main salary being paid in and switches from other providers), so don't get bullied into accounts you don't necessarily want or need.

- If switching your bank account then shop around for the best account for you. Trial a new bank with your current account before you make a switch of all your credits and debits.

3

Managing Your fridge

Your fridge should hold all of your medium term cash savings accounts, everything from your instant access contingency fund to multiple year savings bonds.

Contingency funds

As mentioned in the previous chapter your contingency fund should really be kept in your fridge and not your larder (a savings not current account) not only to protect you from the chance of theft but also to get as much return on it as possible whilst you are not using it. A guideline for contingency funds is to have at least three times your monthly outgoings (if you are working): should anything happen you know that you have yourself covered for a reasonable amount of time. If you are no longer working, you may feel more comfortable having a larger amount of money on instant access but be realistic here, you don't need huge sums on instant access. These types of accounts are not going to give you a particularly good return because of the easy access, so don't let huge sums sit there not earning you anything and losing value with inflation.

Inflation

Ah inflation, now that is an interesting concept that so many people talk about but don't really understand the reality of. So let's cover it now because it is very important to consider when deciding a strategy for your cash.

OK, so in plain and simple terms inflation is the word used to describe the increase in the cost of living. It is calculated by examining the cost of all manner of things such as food, fuel, mortgages, luxury goods etc. There are two indexes used to measure this: the Consumer Price Index (CPI) and the Retail Price Index (RPI). The CPI is a measure of a predetermined 'basket' of consumer goods and services, such as transport, food and medicine. These are averaged to give the CPI figure, which is the main indicator for inflation in the UK. The RPI includes mortgages and council tax in addition to the elements used to measure the CPI.

Most people are aware of inflation but don't really consider the concept when thinking about their savings. If you have £10,000 sitting in a savings account for a year and it's not earning any interest, at the end of the year you may consider it safe because it says £10,000 on your statement but in reality, if inflation is 2.5%, it is actually only worth £9,750. This is because the £10,000 would only buy you £9,750 worth of goods in comparison to the previous year.

This may not seem so bad after one year but let's assume you haven't needed to access that money for 10 years. It's been sitting in the same account all that time and inflation has been a steady 2.5% every year. Just as compound interest can multiply your savings, compound inflation can multiply the effects of inflation. So the value of the goods you could buy with it would only be worth £7,763.30. Theoretically, you have lost £2236.70 – even though your statement still states £10,000.

Now – does that make sense? Probably not! It is a hard concept to get your head around; hopefully this real life explanation will make it easier.

Some time ago…

£1 bought you 3 chocolate bars  with 10p change

Now….

£1 will only buy you one  but with 40p change

If you apply this to all your everyday items and more expensive luxury purchases you can see why it is so important that your money *works* – you need it to grow each year to at least keep pace with inflation. Ideally you want it to grow an amount above inflation so you are also making money. A trap that many fall in to is thinking that keeping lots of money in savings accounts makes it safe. It is safe from fluctuations but with the effect of inflation, if not managed properly, it becomes a sure fire way to actually *lose* money every year without even realising it.

Tax

Before we go on to look at ways of saving tax, it is probably best to confirm something that has shocked many in the past. Yes, you do pay tax on any interest you earn on your savings. It doesn't matter how much or how little you have earned in interest, you will still pay tax on it.

You will pay tax at your current rate, so if you are a basic rate taxpayer you will pay 20% tax on your interest, if you are a higher rate tax payer you will pay 40% and if you are lucky enough to earn over £100,000 then you will be unluckily hit with the additional rate tax of 50%. If you are a married couple and one of you is a basic rate taxpayer and the other a higher, on any joint accounts you will pay 30%. If one of you is a nil rate taxpayer and the other a basic you will pay 10%. This tax is deducted automatically at source unless you are a non-tax payer and you complete an R85 form that ensures the provider does not take it from you.

If you are trying to make your money work as hard for you as it possibly can, one of the last things you want is for tax to be taken off it. A handy little product to use to avoid tax is an ISA.

ISAs (instant savings accounts)

So very simple, yet so seemingly complicated!

A cash ISA is the only way to ensure, if you are a tax payer, that you do not pay tax on your interest. A good idea for start-up savers is to build up contingency funds within a cash ISA. This ensures money you are saving/have saved is working as hard as it can. Once you have filled your cash ISA each year, you can then consider what other type of account is best for you but if you don't have any other savings accounts then that should be your first.

What is an ISA?
Imagine that an ISA is a bucket:

A bucket with a lid so that the tax man cannot get his hand inside to take the tax out!

Into your bucket you are allowed to put **cash** and **investments**.

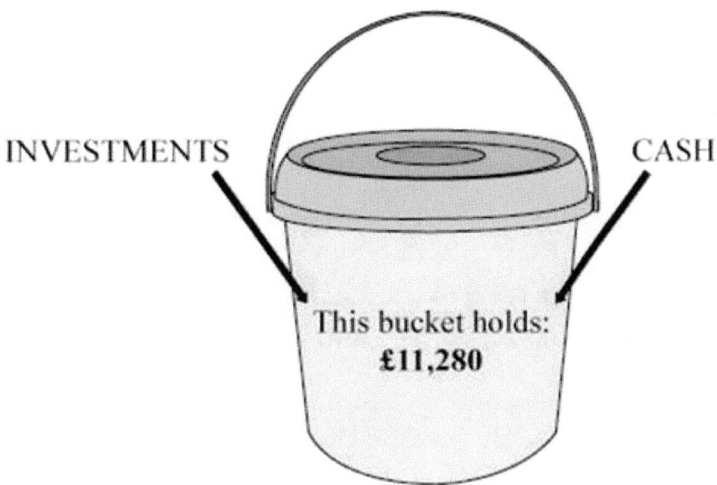

The capacity of your bucket (how much you can put in it) for the 2012/2013 tax year is £11,280. This capacity is referred to as your 'ISA Allowance' and the total allowance of £11,280 has to be split between **cash** and **investments**.

There are three different ways that you can fill your bucket each year:
1. Split it 50/50 between cash and investments and have £5,640 in cash and £5,640 in investments.
2. Split with any ratio you want, as long as you do not exceed the maximum for cash, (which is £5,640) i.e. £3000 cash and £8,280 investments.
3. Fill the entire bucket with £11,280 investments and do not have a cash ISA at all.

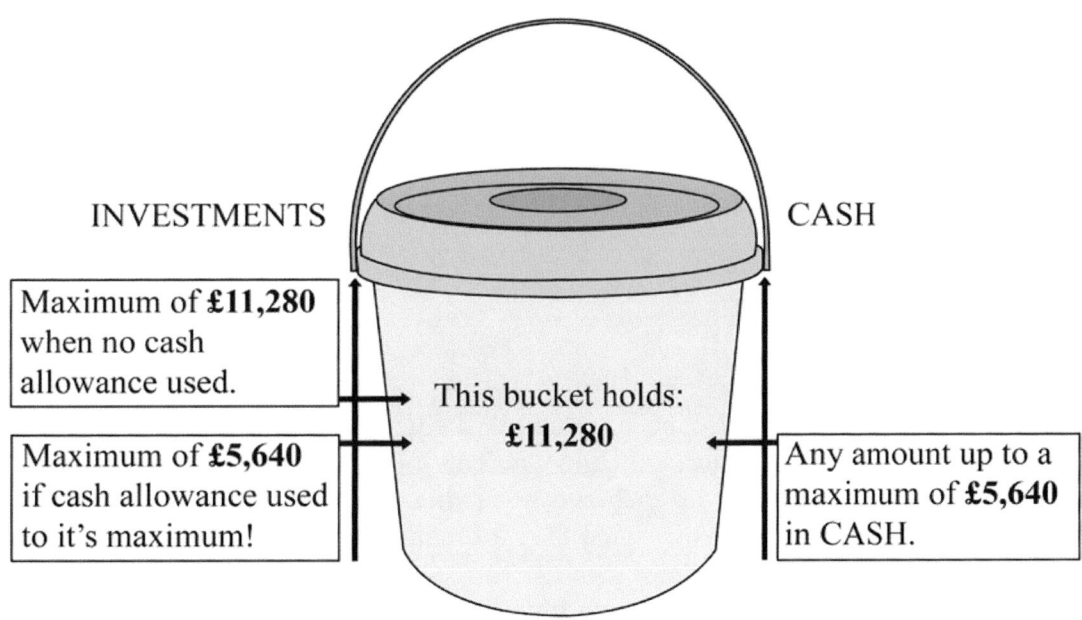

What an ISA does.

It protects your money from tax.

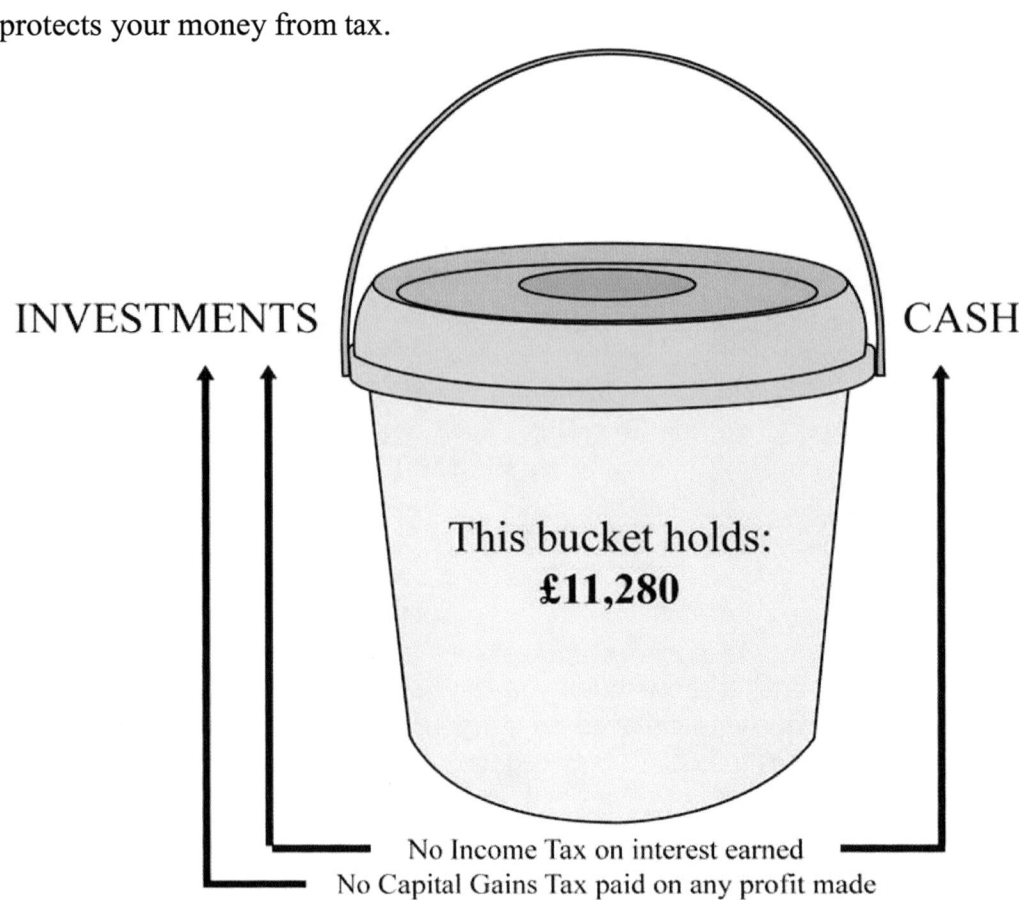

INVESTMENTS   CASH

This bucket holds:
£11,280

No Income Tax on interest earned
No Capital Gains Tax paid on any profit made

If you are only using the cash element of your ISA then you are only taking advantage of half of its tax protection capabilities (because it is only the Income Tax on your interest that you are protecting). You will not see growth on your cash savings that would ever be large enough to incur a Capital Gains Tax charge (an explanation of CGT can be found later in the book).

Please note; you do not have to use the investment element of your ISA but in choosing not to, you are forsaking £5,640 of your money that you could be making tax efficient. I will go into the Investment ISA in more detail in the Freezer section of this book!

Cash ISA buckets

Once you have made a decision on how you will fill your bucket (cash/investments) you will need to find a provider (someone who can look after your bucket for you). If you have decided to use both the cash and investment elements of the ISA these will have to be held separately. This is when they are named as cash ISAs and stocks and shares or investment ISAs. For the rest of the fridge section, I will only be referring to cash ISAs as these are products you keep in your fridge! (Investments ISAs need to be kept in your freezer!)

Continuing on the theme that your cash ISA is a bucket, it is now a slightly smaller bucket with a capacity of £5,640. When you save inside a cash ISA, any interest is tax free and this is added at the end of the tax year to whatever you have in your bucket during the year:

Please note that for the sake of these illustrations the ISA allowance has been kept the same for each year, it is however likely to be increased by the Government each year.

£5,640
+ 3% interest
=
£5,809

At the start of the next tax year you have a choice – you can either add to your existing bucket (ISA) with its current provider, making that bucket expand its capacity:

£5,809
+
£5,640
=
£11,449

Or you can get another bucket with a different provider:

Original bucket
with interest added

£5,809

Provider A

New bucket with new
tax years allowance*

£5,640

Provider B

* ISA allowance may increase

You can continue to do this each year, either topping up an existing bucket to make it
bigger or getting a new bucket with a new provider.

Year 1 ISA getting 3%
each year now worth

£5,983

Provider A

Year 2 ISA getting 3%
now worth

£5,809

Provider B

New bucket with new
years tax allowance*

£5,640

Provider C

*ISA allowance may change

Or

All 3 years ISA's together
in 1 bucket now worth

£17,432.27

How to fill your bucket

There are many different ways to fill your ISA bucket. The best thing that you can do, if you can afford to, is to put the full amount £5,640 in as close to the start of the new tax year as possible. (New tax year begins on 6 April.) This ensures that you will get a full year of interest, tax free. Waiting until the end of the tax year to fill your bucket does not make any sense. (Why leave it in an alternative account paying 20 or 40% tax when it could be inside your ISA saving you that money instead?)

Regular saving is another way you can fill your ISA bucket. If you are going to do this, use a standing order or direct debit straight from your current account into your ISA. Do not save it in a regular savings account with the plan to transfer into the ISA as a lump sum. By doing this you will have lost a whole year's worth of extra savings from tax and this doesn't make any sense! (To make even more money out of saving regularly into an ISA, check out regular savings in the freezer section.)

Should you need to, you can also put ad hoc lump sums into your ISA bucket (as long as you do not exceed the maximum capacity of the bucket for that tax year). If you wish to do this you will need to check with the provider that you can. Some providers do not allow you to put any additional amounts into your ISA once it has been opened – it will often depend upon whether you have fixed it for a set term or not.

Emptying your bucket

If you have put the full allowance into your ISA bucket, the most important thing to know and remember is that once you have taken any money out, you will not be able to put it back in again. This is because you will have used up your 'allowance' for that tax year. Other than this, taking money out of your cash ISA should be no different from any other cash savings account and the terms and conditions will depend upon the provider. If you have allowance left for the current tax year, you will be able to put money back in, as illustrated below.

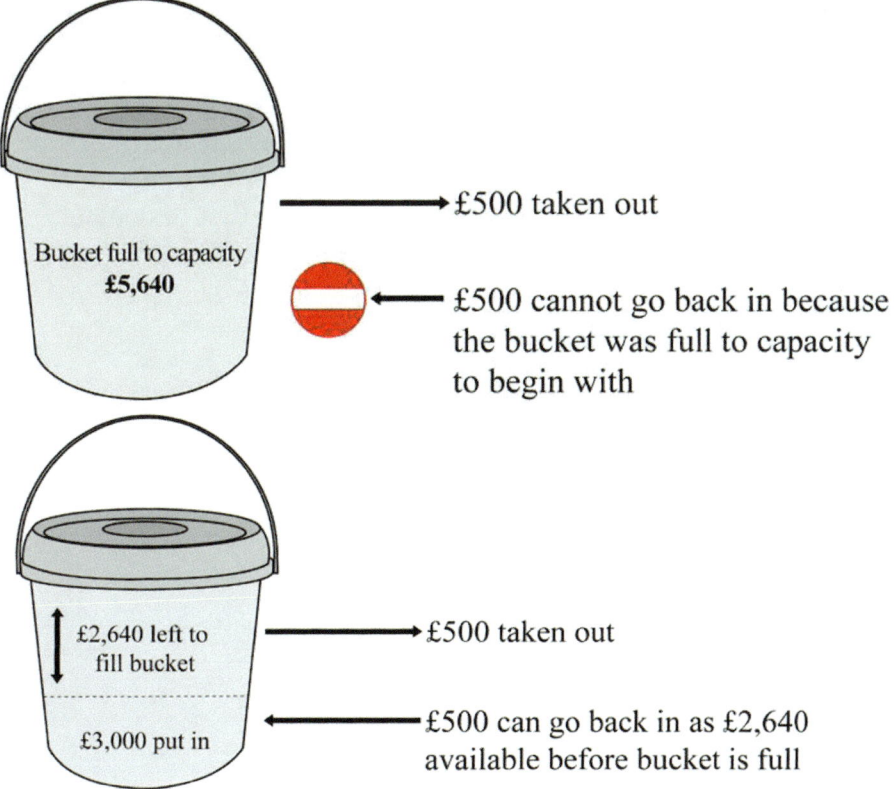

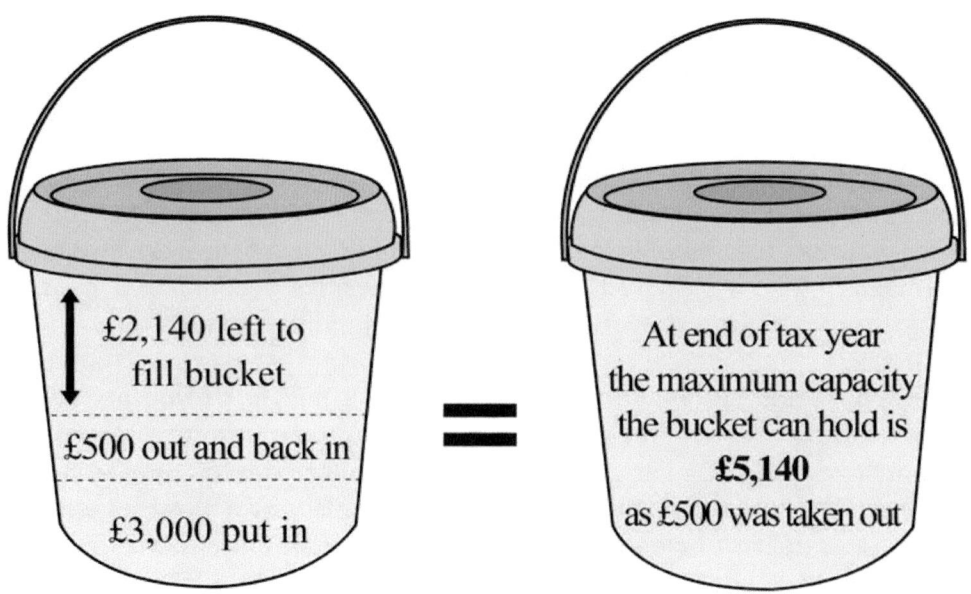

Throwing away your bucket

Should you wish to completely empty your bucket, you are theoretically throwing that bucket away. Once it is empty, it does not exist any more and that year's tax allowance is lost. Having said that, there is no point in keeping £1 in it just to keep it open because once the tax year ends, any new funds will have to be put into the new tax year's bucket.

This is also the same if you have chosen not to put anything in to your bucket for the current tax year. Once the tax year ends, any new funds will have to go into a new tax year's bucket. So the previous years allowance is lost. *If you don't use it you lose it!*

If you have collected many years' worth of ISA buckets think carefully about using the funds out of any of them because you will not be able to replace it once they have gone. Always use any cash that is taxable before you spend funds from your ISAs (see later in the book for a hierarchy of accounts.)

Often people say that they are going to take money out of their ISA or not put money into one because ISAs aren't doing well in comparison to a bank or building society's fixed rate bond. Before you make this decision you must first calculate the comparable interest rates once you have taken the tax payable off the fixed bond.

> ISA = 3.5%   Bond = 3.8%
>
> £10,000 to invest
>
> ISA interest = £350
>
> Bond interest (£380 − 20% Tax) = £304

Not only is it likely to be less for the bond after tax or very close, nobody knows what the future holds with regard to tax. This is why it's so important to build up as much tax efficient holdings as possible (especially heading towards retirement).

Moving your bucket

Whether you have one or many ISA buckets, you can move them to different providers. If you have built up lots of different buckets with different providers, it is also possible to amalgamate them all into one bucket with one provider. However once you have done this, it is not possible to split them back out again.

Whether it is a cash or investment ISA, anyone in finances that you speak to will want you to move all your ISA buckets together under their 'roof' so that they can manage them for you. It is more profitable for them if they are looking after more of your money and convincing people that all their ISAs should be held together is an easy sell for this. Think clearly about your own personal strategy before you do this.

If you decide you do want to amalgamate all your ISAs into one, you must first open an ISA with the new provider; this is so the others can be 'poured' into it. Remember that you will only be able to do this if you have **not** got an ISA for the current tax year (as you can only have one ISA bucket per tax year and your new provider will need to open one for your others to be 'poured' into). The best time to consider any transfers is at the start of the new tax year. This is the time when most of the providers have their best rates available because they want your new business.

It is also very important to remember that you cannot pick up and move your ISA buckets yourself. It must be done as a transfer from one provider to another. If you try to do this by taking money out of one ISA to put it in another one somewhere else, although you will have achieved the move you wanted, you will end up only having one year's worth of allowance instead of two. (Remember that once you have fully emptied a bucket, it vanishes!)

Kicking the bucket!

When you die, all of your ISA buckets vanish. What you had inside them remains but in a taxable account.

Baby buckets

You can purchase Junior ISAs for children holding both cash and investments up to £3600 per year. Once the child reaches 16yrs (cash) and 18yrs (investments) the Junior ISA automatically converts to an adult ISA.

Bonds

The dictionary definition of the word bond is: 'an official paper given by the government or a company to show that you have lent them money that they will pay back to you at an interest rate that does not change'. However there are many different types of bonds and that can make them confusing. Here are a few:

Premium Bonds

A Premium Bond is purchased from the NSI (National Savings & Investments) via the Post Office or on line. It is not a savings account because there is no set rate of interest; instead you have the chance of winning money each month (up to one million pounds). The maximum you are able to put into Premium Bonds is £30,000. You do not pay tax on your winnings so this can be used as an effective tax haven for higher rate tax payers with large quantities of cash.

Many people like to have the full amount in Premium Bonds because they enjoy receiving their winning cheques (usually £25) each month and the money feels safe because the statement always says £30,000 and never deviates from that amount. Two things to consider here: (1) At the end of the year how much return have you actually received? There is a high chance it will be less than a savings account. (2) If you have the full £30,000 you are not able to reinvest any winnings/interest therefore the value of your £30,000 is being eroded by inflation each year. Think about that one if you have had the full amount sitting in Premium Bonds (probably as your contingency fund) for over a decade. How much is that money really worth today compared to when you put it in?

If you have had a large quantity in Premium Bonds for 10+ years, why not analyse it yourself? Work out how much you have had as a return in that time and how much the value of the money is now, if inflation has reduced it by 2.5–3% each year for the last ten years. If you find you're in a negative, have a look in the freezer section for some alternative ideas for where you could put it.

Savings bonds

These are available from banks or building societies and fixed for a set term. The terms for these bonds are six months, one year, two years, three years, four years and five years. It is unusual for them to be fixed for much longer than five years. This is purely a cash bond and will have a fixed interest return that increases with the number of years the term is for. So the longer you tie it in, the higher the return you get and vice versa. You are lending the money to the bank – the longer they know they have it for, the more they can do with it, so the better they reward you for that loan. You will need to check the terms and conditions of each provider's bond individually but be aware that once your money is locked into one of these bonds, you cannot normally access it. With some you can and forgo interest but with others, it's locked up unless you die. Tax at your personal rate (either basic or higher) is paid on these bonds and taken at source.

Income Bonds

These are also cash based bonds and are available from banks and building societies. They are always fixed for a certain period of time and usually 'stepped' so that the income you receive increases every year to keep pace with inflation. If you are a taxpayer you will pay tax on this income. All of the interest that is earned within the account is paid out as your income, so you need to be aware of the effect of inflation on the capital.

Regular Saving

A note on regular saving whilst we are here! Please do not be fooled by the headline rate. Remember that the bank is **not** your friend. The headline rate for a regular saving account is designed to hook and reel you in, normally so they can provide you with additional products. The calculations (too complicated to explain) that banks use to decide what they actually pay as a return on regular savings, means by the end of the year it is substantially less than the headline rate promoted. Before you set up a regular saver be sure to ask the bank for an illustration as to what the actual return will be by the end of the year and base your investing decision on this, not the rate that is advertised.

Regular saver accounts are usually only fixed for a year at a reasonable rate and even if the account continues year after year, chances are the provider will be offering a much better rate on a different account than yours. (Remember how they make their profits). It is not up to the bank to automatically switch you to a better interest account if one becomes available. So don't just let this money go in month after month, year after year, without making sure you are getting the best possible rate on it that you can. Remember – shop around!

If you are planning on doing a regular saving for a longer period of time then have a look in the freezer for a better option.

Strategies for your cash

As already described a very basic strategy for your money is the larder, fridge and freezer with your money divided into short, medium and long term pots. This is the best starting point for someone who is just embarking on their long term savings, as previously described;

The larder = current account(s)

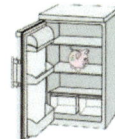

The fridge = cash ISA with contingency fund in it

The freezer = investment ISA or pension

If, however, you have a larger quantity of cash funds that you need to manage then it is important that you have a strategy for your fridge (your cash based savings accounts).

Fridge management

The easiest way to think of this is like the shelves of your fridge. Do you keep all the food on one shelf? No, I didn't think so. In that respect one of the worst things you can do with your money is have it all in one savings account fixed for a set term. The problem with doing this is: (1) if you need to access some, you can't because it is fixed, (2) all of your money matures at the same time, and (3) you have no strategy to ensure you get the best return on your money.

If all your money matures at the same time because it is in one fixed account, you are stuck with whatever interest rates are at that time. This was never much of a problem before when rates were good but this is something people have really struggled with recently when all of their money matured at the same time and the highest option available was only a couple of percent. By fixing all your funds in one account you now also face the concern of how long to tie it up for in case you miss out on rising interest rates by tying it in for too long.

Salad drawer (contingency fund)

You might have one large salad drawer in your fridge but then you may find it gives you a better return to have two. Firstly decide how much you want to have in your overall contingency fund. (Take into account any planned spending that you might want to do over the next year.)

Rather than leaving all this money (especially if it is a larger amount) on instant access where it will earn next to no interest, split it and put half into a six month fixed bond. That way you know the money will be maturing in six months should you need it and in that time it is also earning you a little bit more interest than if it was all on instant access. When it matures, if you find you do not need it, then you can fix it for another six months and so on.

Fridge shelves (savings)

Decide on any planned spending you have over the next five years and ensure that you have this money on the correct shelf (put away for the correct length of time) so that you can use it when it matures. To manage your savings, rather than fixing it all for a set term, break it down as follows:

Bottom shelf – represents a one-year bond

Middle shelf – represents a two-year bond

Top shelf – represents a three-year bond

(Please note: you can add additional shelves to your fridge if you require and fix money for four and five years.)

By managing your fridge this way you know that you have money maturing each year, should you need it for anything. If you don't need it, when it matures you are able to re-fix for the longest amount of time available, earning you the highest amount of interest. It also avoids the problem of all your money maturing at any one time when fixed in one bond. This means you are able to get the best rates available on as much of your funds as possible.

Rotating your fridge shelves

Step one:

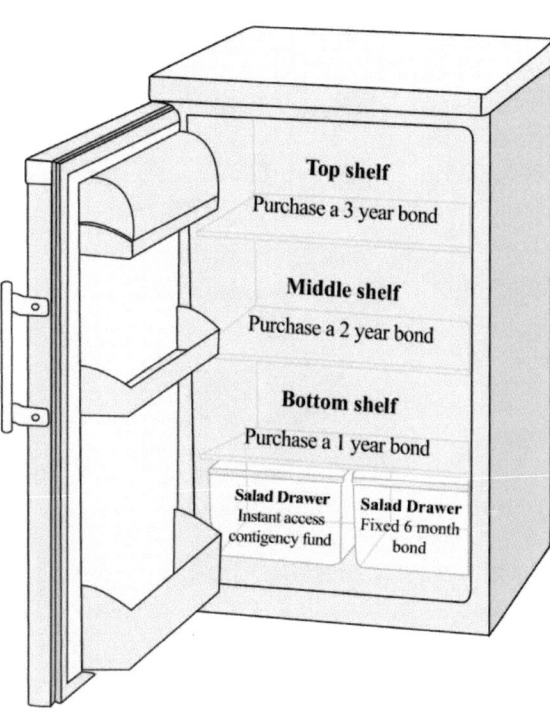

Step two:

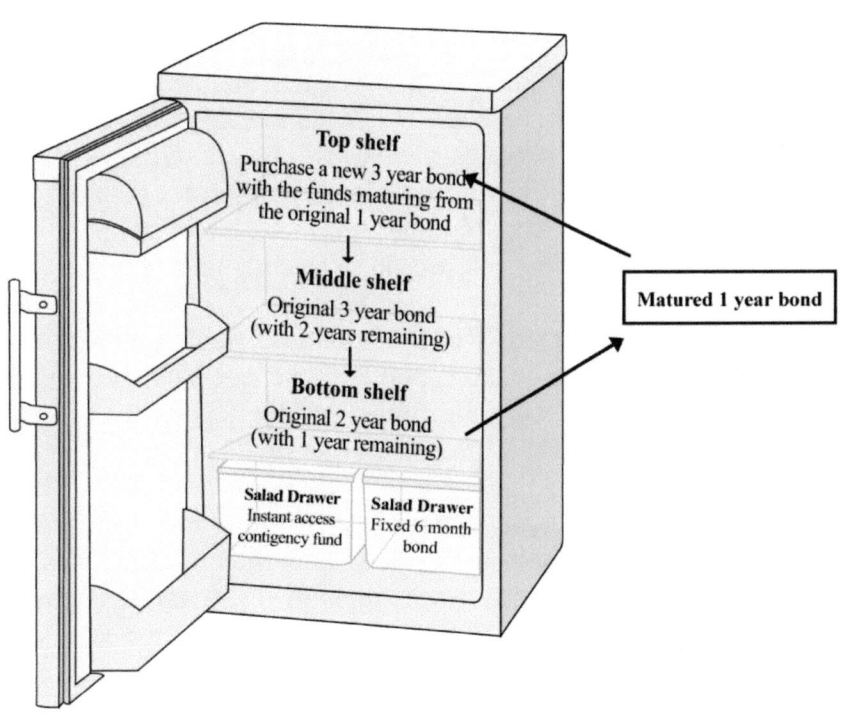

Step three:

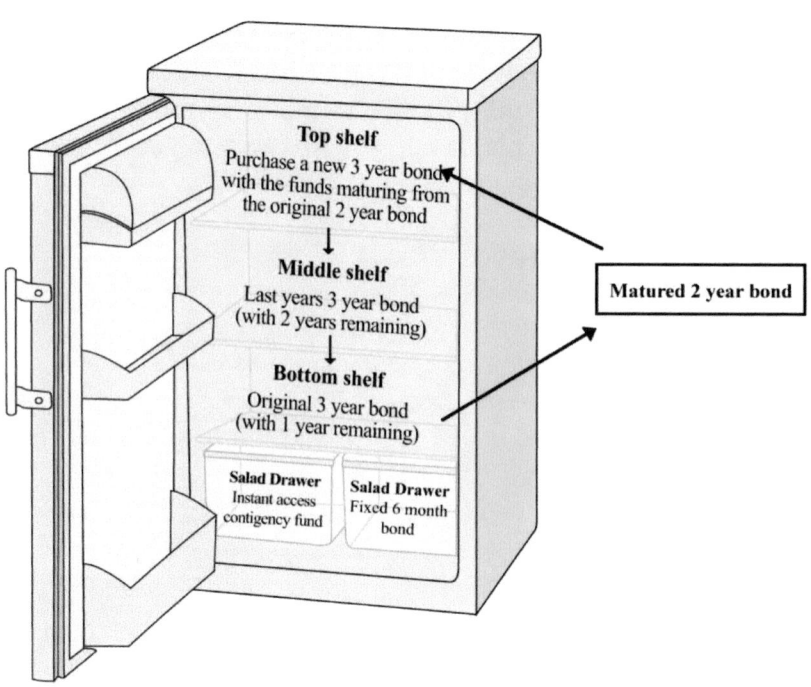

Once you have made the original purchases of one-, two- and three-year bonds (more if you prefer) you will not need to purchase any one- or two-year bonds after this. As the longer term bonds mature they will drop down onto the middle and bottom shelves (as illustrated above). This means each year you are able to take full advantage of the highest possible interest rate available (longest term), knowing that you are not tying all of your money up because there will be another bond maturing in the next year.

Caution
The bank is **not** your friend. If you are to use this strategy with your funds then it is up to **you** to manage it. The bank has to contact you to tell you that your funds are maturing; however the chances are it will be mixed in with so much marketing paraphernalia that you may well miss it. This is all they have to do. It is not in their best interest for you to re-fix your matured funds because once something has matured they can give you next to no interest on it. (Remember how they make their profits.)

There are millions of pounds worth of matured funds that are just sitting in the bank getting nothing in return because people have not bothered to re-fix it, thinking the bank will do it for them. It's your money so you need to make sure you are getting the most out of it.

When you open up a fixed account, it is not a good idea to tick the instruction box for the funds to be automatically reinvested when they mature. This stops you from being able to shop around to get the best rate on the market. (Only do this if shopping around is too much grief for you.)

In order to manage this process effectively and to give yourself enough time to shop around before the bond actually matures, make a note of when each bond matures – with a reminder to start shopping around at least a fortnight in advance. Include such details as:

- The bank the bond is with
- How much you invested
- What percent it was getting
- How long the term was (was it earmarked for any planned spending?)

Please note that you can use your cash ISAs and/or fixed savings bonds to achieve this fridge management. If you are going to use your cash ISAs then you need to purchase a different bucket with a new provider each tax year so that you can fix them for different terms.

During your working years you should aim to use your ISA allowance every year so that you build all of your cash savings up into tax efficient accounts. This ensures that by the time you retire you are not losing valuable interest to tax.

Fridge-freezer
If you want to add another level to your finances and get them to work that little bit harder within your fridge (and you do not need to produce an income from your interest) then you could have the interest from either all or one of your bonds, paid out monthly and saved into a regular savings account.

This way you are making interest on your interest and taking advantage of the slightly higher rate that a regular saver account offers. Please note: this is not recommended if it is interest being produced from an ISA because it is better to let this money grow within the ISA bucket where it is not being taxed!

Fridge freezer example:
Please note this is a basic example, using fictitious interest rates.

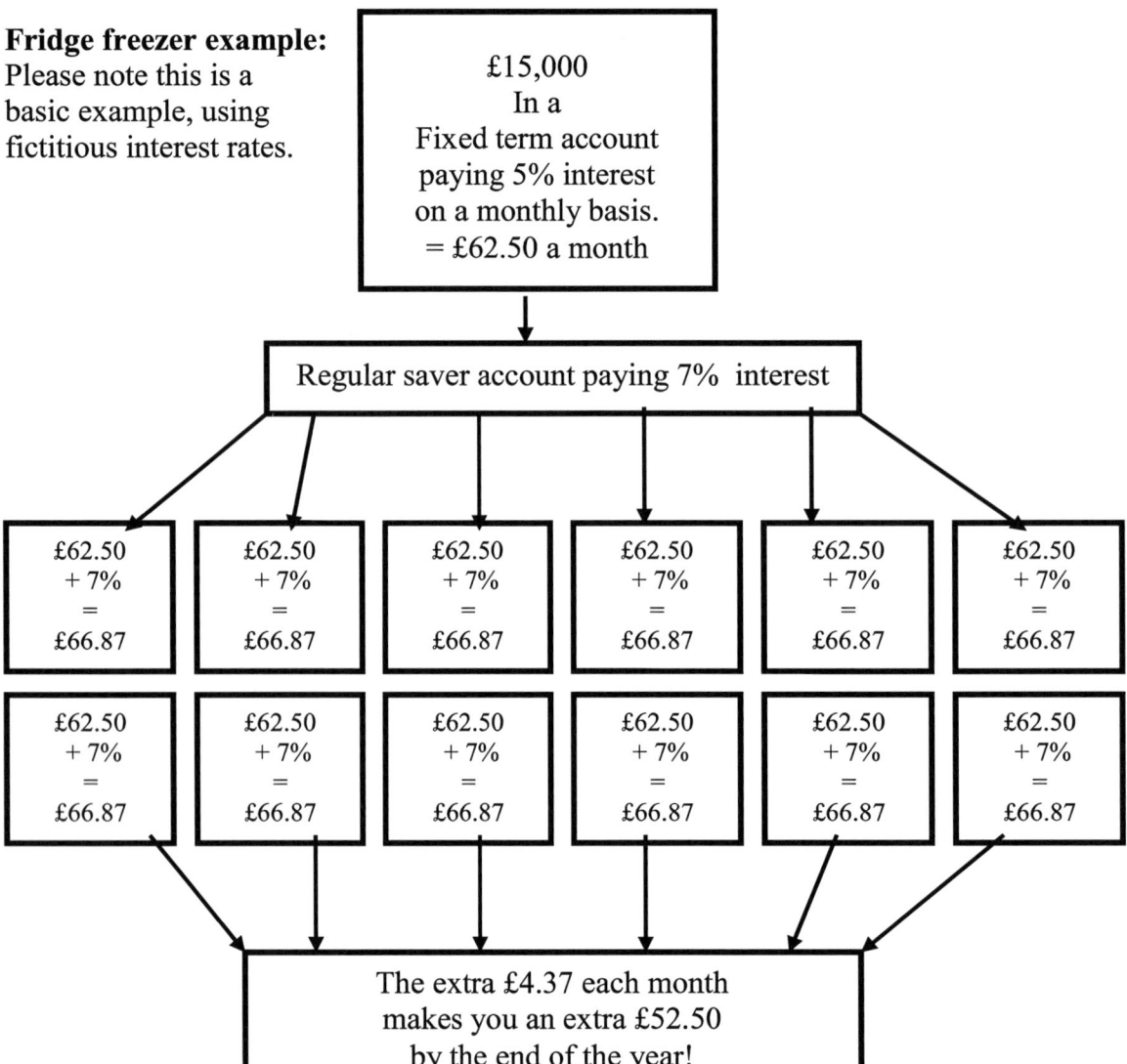

£15,000
In a
Fixed term account
paying 5% interest
on a monthly basis.
= £62.50 a month

Regular saver account paying 7% interest

| £62.50 + 7% = £66.87 | £62.50 + 7% = £66.87 | £62.50 + 7% = £66.87 | £62.50 + 7% = £66.87 | £62.50 + 7% = £66.87 | £62.50 + 7% = £66.87 |
| £62.50 + 7% = £66.87 | £62.50 + 7% = £66.87 | £62.50 + 7% = £66.87 | £62.50 + 7% = £66.87 | £62.50 + 7% = £66.87 | £62.50 + 7% = £66.87 |

The extra £4.37 each month
makes you an extra £52.50
by the end of the year!

Summary of the fridge

- If you want to make your money work as hard for you as it possibly can when kept in cash, by following the techniques outlined in this section, you can get the best out of it that you possibly can!

- Make sure you have an adequate contingency fund so that if you lock money into fixed term accounts you have some you can still access. Split your contingency fund in two and fix half of it for six months so you make a bit extra on it.

- Use your Cash ISA allowance every year to build up tax efficient savings by the time you retire. Manage your savings accounts so that you have money maturing every year and take full advantage of longer term accounts with better interest rates. Use the interest paid monthly on a fixed account to pay in to a regular saver to make that little bit more.

- Most importantly for this section is to remember that it is your job, not the bank's, to manage your accounts. Know when they are maturing and shop around for the best possible rate.

- If you want your money to work even harder and you are able to leave it in the same place for longer than five years, then you need to have it in your freezer. If you do not like the idea of using the freezer then manage your funds within the fridge effectively. Yes that may well mean tying things up for five years but with the strategy outlined for the fridge, this should not be a problem. No matter how old you are, you never know how long you will live, so always have some money working as hard for you as it possibly can in a longer term bond.

4

Managing your freezer

The freezer can arguably be the most important part of your asset management strategy, yet so few people use it because they don't understand it. What makes it worse is when you go to see an adviser for help and are left feeling more confused than when you started.

This last section of The Larder, The Fridge and The Freezer will look at all the different compartments that are available in your freezer (just like your fridge shelves) so that you can either work out for yourself what sections you want to use or at least understand what is being said when you next go to see a professional.

The four main asset classes are; Cash, Property, Stocks and Bonds (not cash bonds as described earlier). Property is only briefly covered in this book and cash has already been discussed so this section will be looking at stocks and bonds.

To understand how cash, bonds and stocks all work together think of them like the M25 motorway.

The hard shoulder

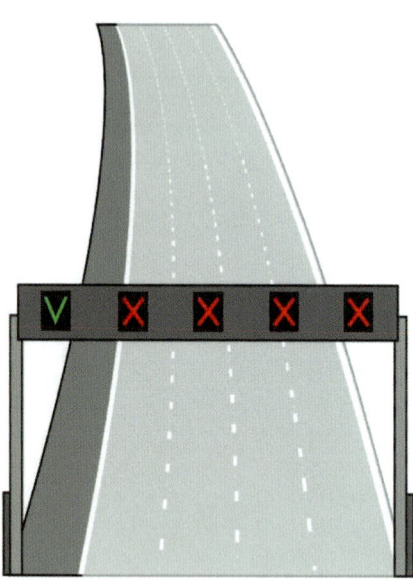

The hard shoulder represents your **cash** (your larder - current account and your fridge - cash ISAs, Premium Bonds and savings bonds etc)

This is because just like sitting on the hard shoulder of a motorway, when your money is in cash it really isn't going anywhere. (By the time it keeps pace with inflation it is just about breaking even and therefore stationary).

With interest rates as they are at the moment and inflation as high as it is, it is more like sitting on the hard shoulder with your handbrake off and you are rolling slowly backwards. Even though you are getting some interest it is not enough to beat inflation so the value of your money is being eroded each year (as previously discussed).

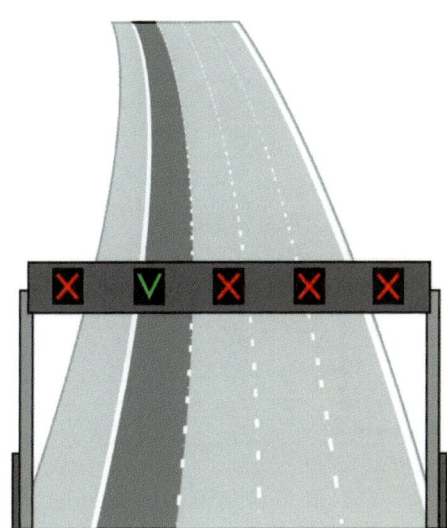

The slow lane represents **fixed interest securities**. (These are not fixed interest cash accounts.)

Fixed interest securities (often known as the **bond market**) comprise two different types of investments: gilts and corporate bonds.

They are represented by the slow lane because they offer a slightly higher return than cash, so you are starting to move a bit quicker (more growth) but there is a reduced chance of having an accident in comparison to the other lanes. (Please note that there is still an element of risk to these types of investments, as there is with all investments).

Let's take a look at each one individually;

Gilts

A gilt is a loan to the Government, much similar to a Premium Bond but with a Premium Bond you have no idea what your return is going to be. Instead you have your numbers and hope that Ernie gives you some winnings. You do not have any set term you hold the Premium Bonds for and you hold them for as long as you like.

Gilts however have a set term and a set interest rate. You can get short, medium and long term gilts and each will give you a different interest rate. They are similar to fixed savings accounts in that the longer the term is for, the higher the interest rate will be.

Gilts are considered to be low risk because the British Government has not defaulted on a payment to date. However, in these unprecedented economic times there have been a couple of incidences with other countries where the ability of the Government to repay the maturing loans has come into question and they have had to receive financial aid to repay them.

Many features of the gilt are the same as a corporate bond, as described below.

Corporate bonds

A corporate bond is the same as a gilt but instead of lending money to the Government you are lending money to a company. This is one of the ways used by companies to raise funds for new products/projects etc. If a company wishes to raise money it will put corporate bonds out onto the bond market (like the stock market). Like gilts they will have a set term and a set rate of return (interest rate), also like Gilts you can get short, medium and long term bonds, with the longer term bonds giving the better rates. The return on a corporate bond is likely to be higher than that on a gilt because there is more risk involved. There is a chance that a company could fold and it is not able to repay the money that has been lent to it. A point to note here is that should this happen, corporate bond repayments do feature on the creditors list, therefore there is a chance of repayment whereas a share would not be repaid at all, thus making them slightly less risky than shares. There are different levels of risk involved with different types of bonds, see credit ratings table later in the book.

An example of a corporate bond

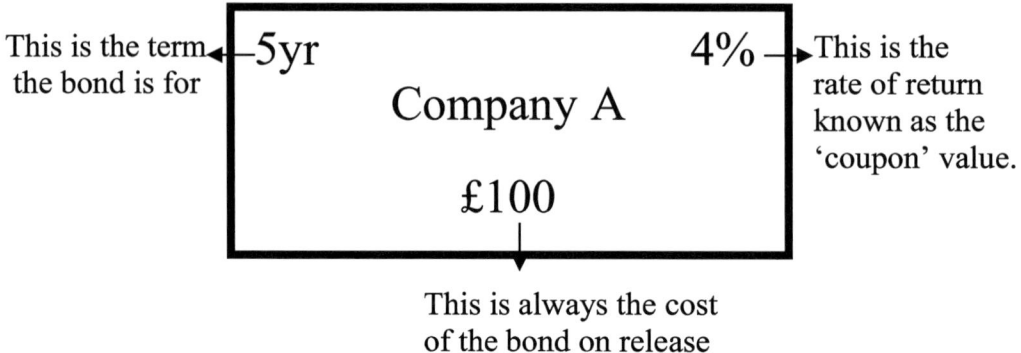

This is the term the bond is for —5yr

Company A

£100

4%— This is the rate of return known as the 'coupon' value.

This is always the cost of the bond on release

Paying interest
These investments are referred to as fixed interest securities because if you purchase a bond with a five year term and a 4% coupon (as pictured above) every year you will get a 4% return on your £100 (£4) and at the end of the five years you will get your £100 back. With this type of investment, if you plan to hold it until maturity and spend the interest, you need to be aware of the effect of inflation on the value of your £100 when the bond matures.

Valuing your Bond
Unlike a savings account (where the value of the money invested remains the same throughout the term), a corporate bond's value fluctuates according to supply and demand within the market. This will not affect you if you plan to purchase the bond on day one and hold until maturity but if you need to sell it before it matures you could make a profit or a loss. (There is an opportunity here to make money if you want to actively buy them whilst they are low and sell them whilst they are high).

It is important to note that if you purchase a bond after its start date and the value is either more or less than the original £100, this will affect the rate of return you make. For example; a bond bought initially for £100 with a 4% coupon is going to pay £4 every year. However the same bond bought later in its term for £115 is still only going to pay £4 a year, therefore giving you a reduced return of 3.5%. Alternatively, if you purchased the same bond for £90 it will continue to pay £4 a year, therefore giving you an increased return of 4.4%.

***Fixed interest*:**

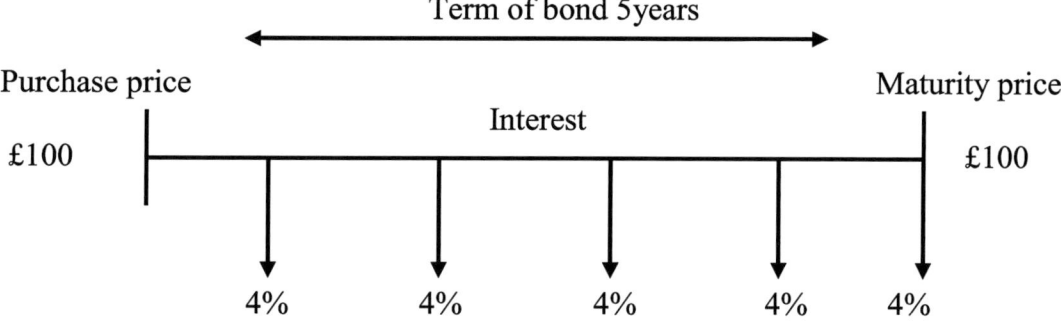

Fluctuating value:

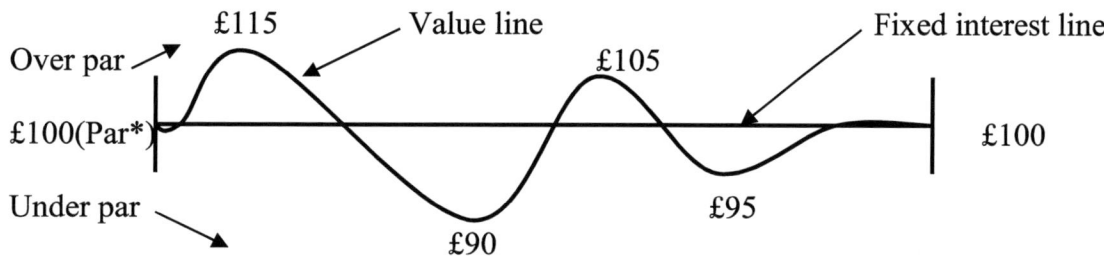

Please note: these figures are just an example to illustrate how the value of a corporate bond can increase and decrease during its term, they are not directly representative of the nature or amounts that these fluctuations can take.

*Par is the original value of the bond ie £100, when the price goes above this it is known as being *over par* and when it goes below this, it is known as being *under par*.

Risk

There is an element of risk involved in any investment. Corporate bonds and gilts are renowned for being less risky than stock market based investments. However within the bond market there are different levels of risk you can take and this will depend upon the credit rating of the company whose bond you are purchasing. There are two main credit rating companies: one is called Moody and the other is called Standard and Poor. These assess the ability of the company (or country if it is a Government issued bond) to be able to repay the loan once it matures.

This rating will determine the level of return you get on the bond and how much the cost might fluctuate during its term. For example a bond rated as a triple A on purchase that is downgraded during its term to a single A will fall below par as demand for it drops.

The ratings are split into two; investment grade bonds and non investment grade or junk bonds. The higher the grade the bond has, the less risk you are taking in lending that company money and therefore the less return you will get. The lower the grade, ie junk bonds, the more risk you are taking so the higher the return. An easy way to think of this is the bigger the company (ie big named household brand) the higher the rating will be and the smaller the company (ie small startup internet firm) the lower the rating will be. A good strategy for managing your risk/return within the bond market is to diversify and have various different bonds at different credit ratings.

Credit rating table:

	Moody's	Standard and Poor's
Investment-grade bonds		
Highest quality bond	Aaa	AAA
High quality	Aa	AA
Upper medium grade	A	A
Medium grade	Baa	BBB
Non-investment grade (junk) bonds		
Lower medium	Ba	BB
Low grade	B	B
Poor quality	Caa	CCC
Most speculative	Ca	CC
Bankruptcy petition filed	C	C
In default	C	D

Bond strategy

Corporate bonds can be a great way to produce an income – especially if they are held within an investment ISA, as the income that is produced is then not taxed. You can purchase corporate bonds individually via a stock broker. Brokers will have a minimum amount (in the thousands) that you have to purchase for each company and there will be costs involved in the purchase. Alternatively, you can buy them within a pooled fund which will have a much smaller minimum requirement to purchase (in the hundreds). Pooled funds are discussed later in the book. Both ways are good for producing an income and both can be held within an ISA.

The following strategy is for individual company bonds (not pooled investments) and would need to be purchased and set up for you by a stockbroker.

Much similar to the strategy used for your fixed term accounts you can set up what is known as a bond ladder. It is necessary to note here that corporate bonds bought singularly will pay out once a year; therefore the structure of your bond ladder is somewhat more intricate than the shelves for your fridge to ensure regular payments.

An example bond ladder

Designed to make quarterly payments, income produced is based on £15,000 of each bond being held (these figures are examples only to illustrate the variety)

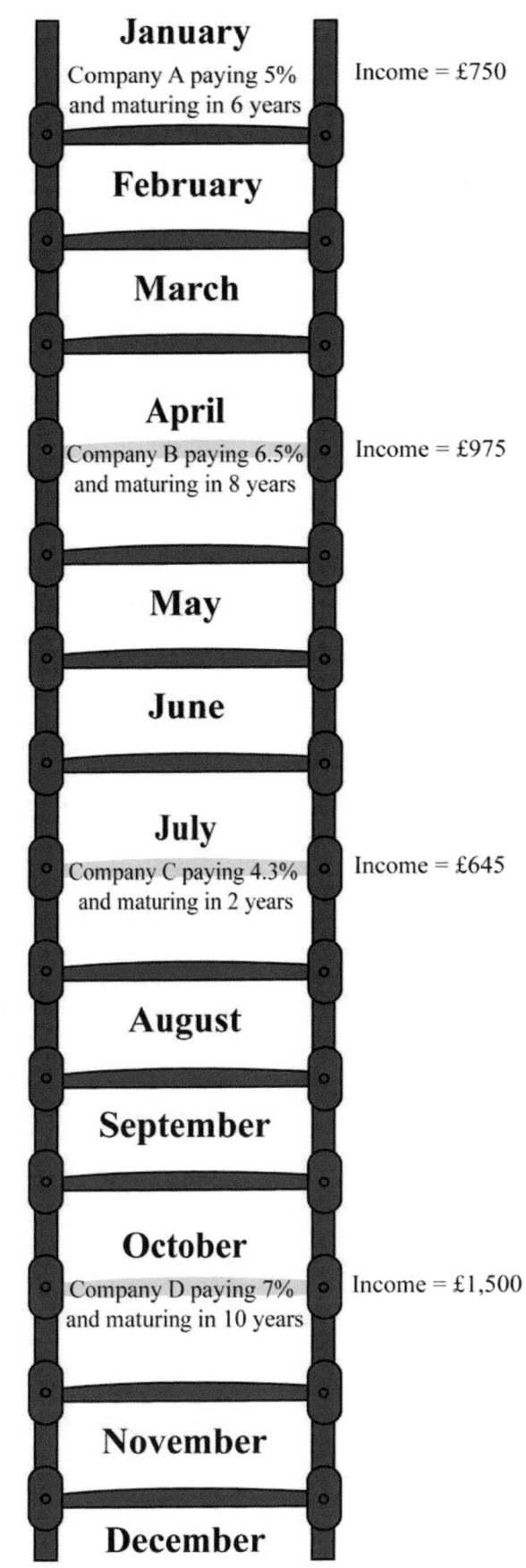

January
Company A paying 5% and maturing in 6 years — Income = £750

February

March

April
Company B paying 6.5% and maturing in 8 years — Income = £975

May

June

July
Company C paying 4.3% and maturing in 2 years — Income = £645

August

September

October
Company D paying 7% and maturing in 10 years — Income = £1,500

November

December

The great thing about a bond ladder in comparison to fixed term cash savings is the flexibility and variety it can offer. When creating your bond ladder you can select bonds with different dates for payments, various terms before maturity, different interest rates etc. Don't forget that if you buy them under par the return (interest) you get is higher than the stated coupon value, as well as the profit made when they mature at their original cost of £100. For example if you purchased 150 of a bond with each one priced at £95 (£14,250), when they mature you will make an extra £750 because each will be repaid at £100 each (£15,00).

A word of caution

Two things to consider if you want to purchase bonds are: (1) that the company could fold and you could potentially lose all the money invested in that particular bond and (2) the effect of inflation on the capital used to purchase the bonds if the income produced is not reinvested in some way for growth.

Avoid buying bonds all in the same industry, for example if you bought all bank issued bonds and the banking system collapsed you could lose all your money. If you have diversified it as much as possible and own some health company, some food retailer as well as some banking issued bonds, if there is any problems with one particular type of industry, you have reduced your exposure to that risk. Until Lehman Brothers in the States folded, the prospect of large companies with high credit ratings being any kind of risk for corporate bond holders was unthinkable but now it is a realistic risk that needs to be considered and planned for.

Creating growth from your bond ladder

If you do not need to create an income from your bond ladder then a great way to manage your money and make it work harder for you is to reinvest the income produced and buy shares. A bond ladder can create further funds for investment if you are no longer working and want to continue actively investing in the stock market.

Derivatives

A quick word about derivatives as they are growing in popularity with banks as a way to provide low risk, 'capital protected' investments. A derivative is not a share but another type of loan. However, unlike corporate bonds or gilts, derivatives do not give you set return on the loan you are making. Instead the return is 'derived' from the growth of something else. That something else (with mainstream investing) is usually the FTSE 100 or an alternative stock market; however it can be set against the potential growth of anything.

For example:

If a company wants to borrow £100 for the next five years, instead of determining a 5% return on your £100 at the start (like a corporate bond), they state they will give you the relative growth of the stock market over that period instead. So the gamble for the investor is that the stock market may grow or it may be at a loss during that period. This means that, similar to shares, the return at the beginning is unknown. However unlike shares, there is a contract that ensures the company at the very least will return the initial £100 investment.

This gives you the added security of knowing if the market drops during that period you will at least get your original money back (similar to bonds).

So a derivative is similar to a share in the unknown quantity of return you may get but also similar to a corporate bond in that you will at least get back your initial investment. This does lend them to being a beneficial investment for the more cautious investor but I hasten to add that there is of course a catch. The company borrowing the money is most likely to cap the amount of growth they will pay. So if the stock market grows 70% you will only ever get the highest level of the cap (likely to be around 35 - 40%.)

These products are most often known as 'capital protected' investments and extra care should be taken when investing these inside an ISA. They have a specific maturity date and when they mature if you have not instructed the provider to reinvest them into another capital protected product, when it matures it is transferred back into cash and you will lose the ISA wrapper it was invested in because you cannot transfer from investments to cash within an ISA. The alternative to stop that happening would be to arrange reinvestment into alternative funds before it matures. The key here is to take action before it matures and is too late.

Back onto the motorway
Back on to the motorway and we have now looked at the hard shoulder and the slow lane. These lanes are referred to as 'loan' investments because in this category you are making your money work for you by lending it out to other people and receiving a return on it in the form of interest. Theoretically taking it out from underneath your mattress (where it is not making any money at all) and lending it to either the bank/building society when you put it in cash savings, the Government when you buy gilts or companies when you buy corporate bonds.

Hardshoulder	Slow Lane
Any cash savings	Gilts and Corporate Bonds
Fixed and variable accounts	
~	~
Lent to the bank or building society	Lent to either the Government or a company

An alternative to 'loan' investments are 'own' investments. Own investments are when you buy shares in a company and become a part owner of it. When you buy shares you are buying your right to that company's future profits. The rest of the motorway is dedicated to 'own' investments, (different types of shares).

Before you run to the hills in fear and panic, there are a few things to consider with regards to the stock market that can make it seem much less scary and in fact easier to manage than you may have been led to believe.

Understanding the stock market

1) The stock market reacts more to emotion than it does to anything else. Unfortunately in this day and age the media is pretty much responsible for this. If they continuously report bad news, whether it is scare mongering headlines directly linked to the performance of the stock market or general bad news about the economy etc it creates a feeling of unease within the country. As people begin to feel uneasy, they start to take their money out of the stock market (for fear of a crash) and move it in to safer investments such as bonds and cash. This action in itself lowers the value of the shares on the market thus causing the market value to drop. As it drops, the papers report the losses and more people (yes we are more like sheep than you can ever imagine when it comes to investing) start to take their money out.

This becomes a self-fulfilling prophecy, driving the market value further and further down as more and more people take their money out. Until eventually, the media starts to report good news again and as this slowly filters through (very slowly because the media don't like to report good news) people tentatively start to move their money back in and in doing so it gradually pushes prices back up. When the market is doing really well again everyone wants a slice of the action so they put more money in and this drives prices up even further, until the cycle begins all over again!

2) The stock market is the only market people want to buy at full price. If you went to a garage to buy a car and it was half the price it should be, you would probably get done for biting off the hand of the salesman in your eagerness to get it before he changed his mind! This is the same with everything in life – we love a bargain. Even those who can comfortably afford full price still like to feel they are getting a good deal. So why is it when the market is at rock bottom and shares are half the value they should be (meaning you can get twice as many for your money), nobody buys them? Instead waiting until they are right back at full price again (giving you less for your money). Everybody knows the term, 'buy low, sell high' but it is only a very few investors who actually do this and these are the ones who make all the money.

3) You need to treat the stock market in the opposite way to your emotional reaction to it. If you are scared – invest more, if you are confident – invest less. When everyone else is investing – hold tight. When no one else is investing – plough your money in. How many other ways are there to say it? It takes courage to go against the grain but it is an almost guaranteed way that in the long run you will make a tidy profit.

4) Face your fear, hold your nerve. When the stock market looks like it might be heading down (unless you need your money in the near future) don't take it out. By doing this you crystallise the loss that you have already experienced (and chances are

you will also miss the growth as it creeps back up again). Also when you repurchase (if at all) it is likely to be once the market is higher than your original investment (you will want to be absolutely sure all is ok before you put any money back in) and this will result in an even bigger overall loss because you are now getting less for your money. (Don't forget the commission you would have paid for both the sale and repurchase of your investments).

5) They say two things in life are guaranteed, death and taxes. Well I say that there are three: death, taxes and the fact that your investments will go down in value at some point during the term that you hold them for. If you can prepare yourself for this from the outset it will enable you to manage your own expectations and not worry (too much) about your investments once you have made them. If you are going to do long term investing, you need to invest and forget.

Finally, I would like to take this opportunity to clarify a grey area when it comes to discussing equity based investments or stocks and shares as they are commonly known. Stocks and shares are in fact the same thing. They are just different ways of describing the overall investment. If you use the term stocks you are referring to any company in general but when you use the term shares, you are making reference to a specific company. For example; 'I invest in stocks' (general) compared to 'I own shares in Company A' (specific). However, you're not mad and yes confusingly they are often referred to as stocks and shares!

Back on the M25....

The middle lane

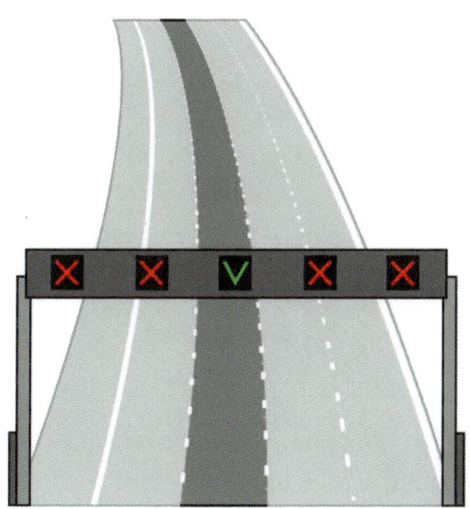

The middle lane on the motorway is representative of a type of share called a **growth and income** share. This share is arguably the lowest risk of all the different share classes.

The income that this share produces makes it a steadier and therefore less risky share to hold than the others that are available.

Owning a growth and income share is much like driving down the middle lane on a motorway. You are travelling quicker than the slow lane but you're still going along at a nice steady pace, so not too much chance of an accident.

Growth and income shares

When comparing a corporate bond and a growth and income share, the differences and similarities are;

A corporate bond has a **set term** until it matures, a **coupon rate** instructing on what interest you will earn until maturity and the price at release is a set £100.

When you purchase a share, there is NO SET TERM that you hold that share for. It is based purely on how long the company is in existence for or how long you wish to hold the share for (shares do not mature.) If you are ever faced with a maturity date on your investment, this is not the actual shares that are maturing but the type of product they are being held in.

The next big difference is the price, there is **no set price** for shares and they can be any price from 1p upwards to purchase and or sell. This value can fluctuate according to the company and demand in the market for its share. Shares do not mature and as there is no set price to purchase (like there is for a bond) when you own shares you will not know how much you will get back until you sell them. It is important to note that this can be more, less or the same as what you originally paid for them. This risk factor is the element of buying shares that most investors fear. However, although there is the risk that you could get back less; there is also the benefit that you could get back more, at an amount over and above inflation, thus giving you a profit.

Finally the one thing that is the same with growth and income shares as corporate bonds is the element of income produced. growth and income shares pay out **dividends**. A dividend is exactly the same as interest but because you are now a part owner of the company (shareholder) instead of a lender to the company, it has a different name. An additional benefit to being a part owner rather than a lender is that you are likely to get a higher rate of return as your reward for investing in that company. So where you might get 4% on a corporate bond, you may well get 5% or more as a dividend payment with the same company.

Dividends

A dividend can be used for two things: (1) to create more growth and (2) to produce an income (please note that there is a 10% tax charge on all dividend payments and no tax products are available to shield from this charge – not even an ISA).

It is the payment of the dividend that makes the growth and income share a lower risk than all the other share types. Although you still have the risk of a fluctuating value and no definitive cash in price, this is counteracted by the steady income that is produced.

There are different ways to manage this type of share according to what you want from it. If for example, you do not want to take the dividend as an income then you can purchase what is known as an accumulative share. This will automatically use your dividend payment to purchase you further shares in that company. By doing this you are increasing your overall holding in that company and therefore also your opportunity for growth. If you need to have the income paid out, you would purchase a distribution share. The income that is then produced can either be used for everyday living expenses or if saved into a cash savings account it can balance out the risk of any fluctuations in the share value.

Options for Dividend Payments

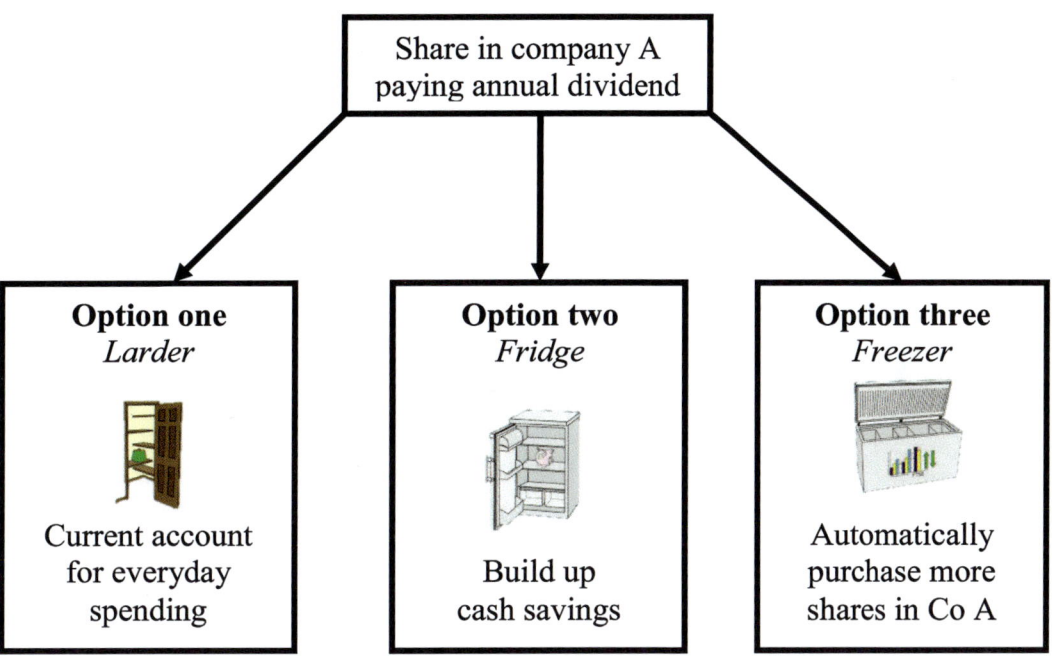

Much of a company's financial strength is based on their ability to pay dividends, so it is not something they like to default, delay or cancel. Doing this can have a negative impact on the share price because demand for that share will reduce. If a company's share price is devalued then this reduces the overall value of the company itself. So it is quite unlikely that if you purchase a growth and income share the company will stop paying the dividend (unless there is an unforeseen catastrophe).

You should also note here that an additional benefit to having dividends create part or all of your income is that when times are good a company is likely to increase their dividend payment each year. This increase can be at an amount that is way above inflation, thus ensuring that your income keeps up with the increasing cost of living. (Something a fixed income cash bond or corporate bond would not be able to do).

So far on our trip round the motorway we have made it out into the middle lane, driving reasonably steady with not too much chance of an accident. So what happens if you want to go faster and get to your destination a bit quicker?

Loan Investments		Own Investments
↘ ↓		↓
Hardshoulder	**Slow Lane**	**Middle Lane**
Any cash savings		Growth and Income Shares
	Gilts and Corporate Bonds	
Fixed and variable accounts		
~	~	~
Lent to the bank or building society	Lent to either the Government or a company	Bought from a variety of companies

The fast lane

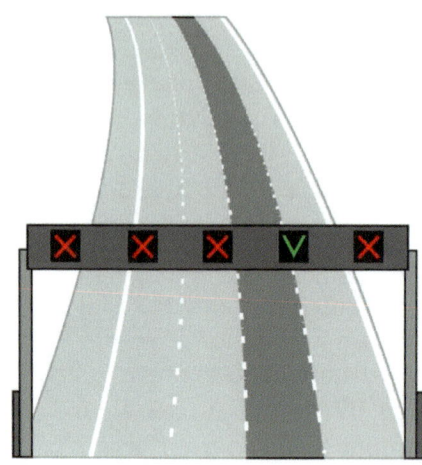

The fast lane of the motorway is representative of a type of share called a **growth share**.

With this share you are starting to take a bit more risk and just like the fast lane of the motorway there is an increased chance of having an accident.

However just like on the motorway, you are going to travel further because you are going that little bit faster. With these shares you will see more growth and potentially in a shorter amount of time than with the growth and income shares.

Growth Shares

When you buy a growth share the company does not pay out any of its profits in dividends like the growth and income share companies do. Instead they reinvest all of the profits back into the company to assist in its overall growth. Therefore when you own growth shares you will see the value of the share increase faster and by a larger amount than the growth and income share. Although this produces greater growth for the investor, it does of course increase the risk because you do not have that steady income stream to balance any losses out with.

Back on the motorway

Our trip round the motorway is nearly complete but what if you are feeling a bit reckless and want to put your foot down or you need to overtake that annoying car that won't get out the fast lane?

Loan Investments		Own Investments	
Hardshoulder	**Slow Lane**	**Middle Lane**	**Fast Lane**
Any cash savings Fixed and variable accounts	Gilts and Corporate Bonds	Growth and Income Shares	Growth Shares
~	~	~	~
Lent to the bank or building society	Lent to either the Government or a company	Bought from a variety of companies	Bought from a variety of companies

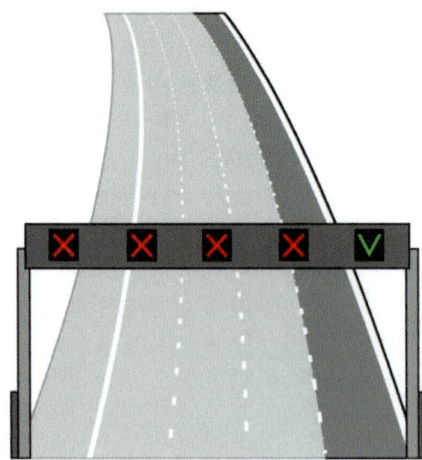

The super fast lane of the motorway represents what are known as aggressive shares.

These are the shares that get all the bad press! When you hear someone say 'I invested in Company X and lost all my money' the chances are they invested in aggressive shares without realising.

These are high risk shares but they also give the opportunity for a high return. So you are travelling much faster down the motorway but with a lot more chance of an accident.

Aggressive shares

Aggressive shares are ones in companies that are considered very high risk, for example this could be a small start up company (like the lower graded corporate bonds, known as junk bonds) or long established companies that look like they might go to the wall but have a new management strategy in place to assist recovery. Either way, the share is likely to be cheap because no one knows for sure what the future for that company holds and the risk you take is that if that company takes off or recovers you are going to do extremely well and see a big return on your money. If however, it collapses then you could potentially lose the lot. The big comparable difference between growth and income and growth shares is that these are likely to be big well established blue chip companies who plod along, giving a steady return and growth year on year. Whereas aggressive shares are the frisky little start up companies with loads of energy and an uncertain future.

Buying aggressive shares is a really easy thing to do without even being aware that you are doing so. This is why so many people who invest in shares (on a whim without any guidance) go wrong and lose all their money. We are all naturally led by greed and if you were given £10,000 and told this is yours to invest, chose what you like on the stock market, you would be highly likely to choose the share that has returned 30-40% in comparison to one that has returned 5-8%.

Now you could say that is only because its not your money and you are happy to take a risk with it but if you had a spare £10,000 of your own and there was a chance you could make £3000 in a year compared to say £600, the majority of people would go for the riskier £3000, thinking it made that last year, chances are it will again this year. If that company then goes to the wall and you lose all your money you will have had your fingers burned and consider all investing to be bad news, choosing in future to stick to cash and let it be eaten away by inflation instead. If, however, you didn't take that initial risk and instead chose the steady option and over the next five years you got £3000 growth (£600 a year), you'd be a very happy investor who would likely carry on making sensible and profitable investments for the rest of your life – beating inflation and making a profit.

A really great example of this in reality was the Dot Com bubble. People threw money into these tiny little start-up companies thinking it would make them rich overnight. They didn't realise that not only were these high risk companies because they were just starting up but this was a double risk because it was also a new industry for the stock market to get to grips with. All this money ploughing into the stock market made share prices swell but when it all collapsed the negative impact was on everything, even well established companies. The crash made people frightened that they would lose all their money no matter where it was invested, so they took it out and as described before, that sent share prices down.

A final look at the M25

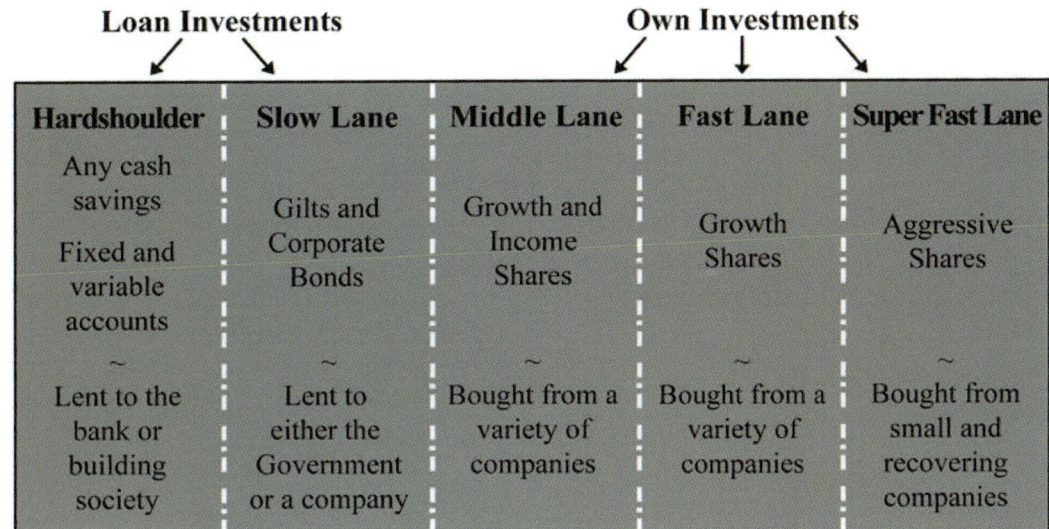

Travelling on the motorway

When you go onto the motorway you don't just pull up on the hard shoulder and sit there for a bit (well at least I hope not!) Instead you tend to use the different lanes according to your journey. Even if you are a cautious driver who prefers to stick in the slow lane you sometimes have to at least go out into the middle lane to overtake the odd lorry. If you are steady driver who likes to sit in the middle lane (yes, you know who you are) you also have to occasionally drift out into the fast lane to overtake that damn Rover that is going even slower than you are but is frustratingly still sitting in the middle lane! If you are a fast driver who likes to keep pace down the super fast lane for the whole of your journey you still have to cross the other lanes to get there, even if you don't spend a lot of time in them.

Its OK, you haven't just started reading a Jeremy Clarkson rant about middle lane drivers! Investing is exactly like driving on a motorway and by seeing it like this it will help you to manage your own expectations of what you can expect from the type of investments that you have.

The traffic jam

The only time the lanes on the motorway get mixed up and you end up going faster in the hard shoulder than those that are stationary in the fast lane is when there is a traffic jam. Investments can work like this in different economic environments as they all react differently. For example, when the stock market is doing well, the bond market tends to do less well because demand for secure investments drop, so prices go down. (Remember the example of fluctuating values earlier in the book). However when the stock market goes down, demand for bonds goes up, as people move their money into safer investments. This is similar with cash and the bond market. When interest rates on cash go down, demand for bonds (paying a slightly higher return) goes up, so their value increases but when interest on cash goes back up again, demand for bonds drops and so does their value.

The relationship between stocks and bonds

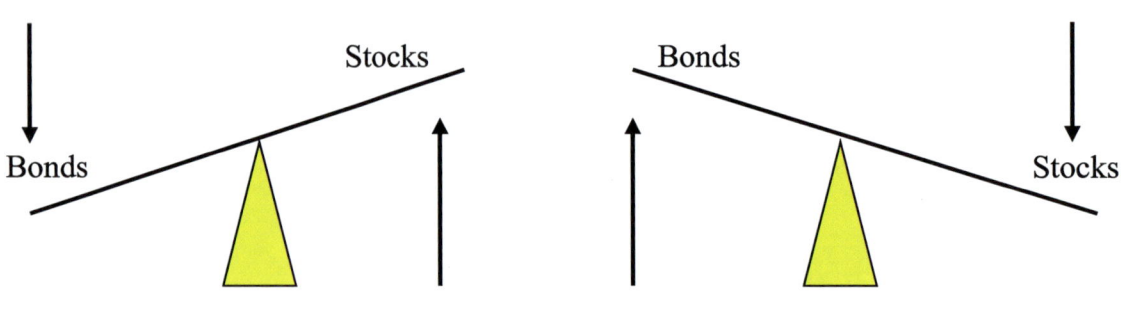

The relationship between bonds and cash

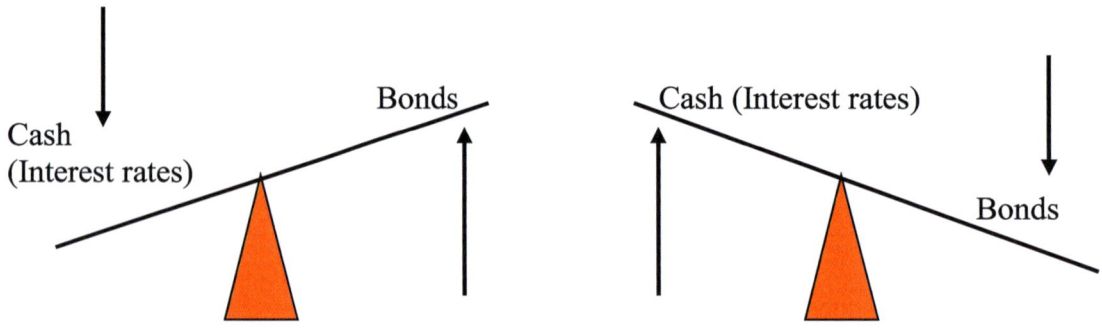

Because all the different asset classes work for and against each other like this, it is important to have some money in each one (cash, bonds & stocks). The old adage of 'don't keep all your eggs in one basket' is a good one to consider.

The cautious driver

If you are a cautious driver/investor who would prefer to stay in the slow lane for the whole of your journey then it will take you an awfully long time to get anywhere. You will therefore need to hop into the middle lane occasionally. As a low risk investor you would probably say that if you are going to invest then you would only want to do it in the slow lane/bond market but by limiting yourself to one type of investment like this you are almost putting yourself at more risk. If bond prices drop you have nothing to back you up. Therefore even as a cautious investor it is necessary to invest in both the bond market and at least growth and income shares in the stock market. This balances you out so you have funds in each of the different asset classes without taking lots of risk. It also means you are likely to get a better return on your money overall.

The middle lane driver

As a middle lane driver/medium risk investor you happily spend time in both the slow and middle lane, (invested in both bonds and growth and income shares) but using the fast lane is something you don't really like to do, much similar to the prospect of investing in the higher risk growth shares. It is important though, just like you have to use the fast lane to do the odd bit of overtaking, that you have some money invested in growth shares. This increases your chance of growth but also represents you more accurately as a medium risk investor.

The fast lane driver

The fast and super fast lane driver is the adventurous investor. In a hurry to get to your destination, you are happy to stay put in both of the outer lanes (invested in growth and aggressive shares). You like to see big and quick growth on your money and you are happy to take the necessary risks to get there. This is all well and good but what happens when there is a traffic jam and that blasted Rover is now way ahead of you, happily doing thirty in the slow lane whilst you, in the super fast lane, are at a standstill? Wish you were over there now don't you? This is exactly the same with investing, even if you are happy to take lots of risk and want your money in the riskier investments and regard the bond market as a 'drag' on your return. It is necessary to hold some of your investments in this lane because there will be times when the stock market goes down and the bond market goes up. By already holding investments in this market, you will not need to sell any of your stock at a loss to temporarily move into more secure investments because you will already have some there. This means you can leave it all where it is. As an overall strategy for your investments this will give you a better return in the long run than buying and selling in reaction to the market.

Which lanes to drive in? (Assessing your risk)

The percentage of holdings you should have in each different asset class will depend on how much risk you want to take. You can either decide for yourself whether you think you are a low, medium or high risk investor or do a specially designed quiz (much like a personality quiz) that can analyse your answers and decide for you. There are lots of different quizzes you can take on line if you type 'risk tolerance questionnaire' into a search engine. It is best to take a few from different sites rather than just relying on one as this will give you a better idea of what your general attitude to risk is. You can then purchase your investments in line with this to build the yourself the correct 'risk profile' portfolio for you.

Your investment journey

A lifetime of investing is a journey and just like travelling on the motorway, it depends how fast you want to go, as to how quickly you arrive at your destination. The more risk you take with your money, the more growth you will have (the further you travel). Consider the first journey you take to be from when you start work (location South Coast) to when you retire (location Scottish border), how quickly do you want to arrive at the Scottish border/retirement? Would you like to get there early so you can relax for longer or are you happy to plod along and have some stop offs along the way with less time to relax once you get there? Scotland/retirement is your second investment journey and you need to consider what you would like to do once you get there. Will you be happy to potter about on local A roads? Or do you want to travel even further and visit the Shetlands? All of these decisions need to be considered when you are deciding what lanes of the motorway you plan to use on your journey.

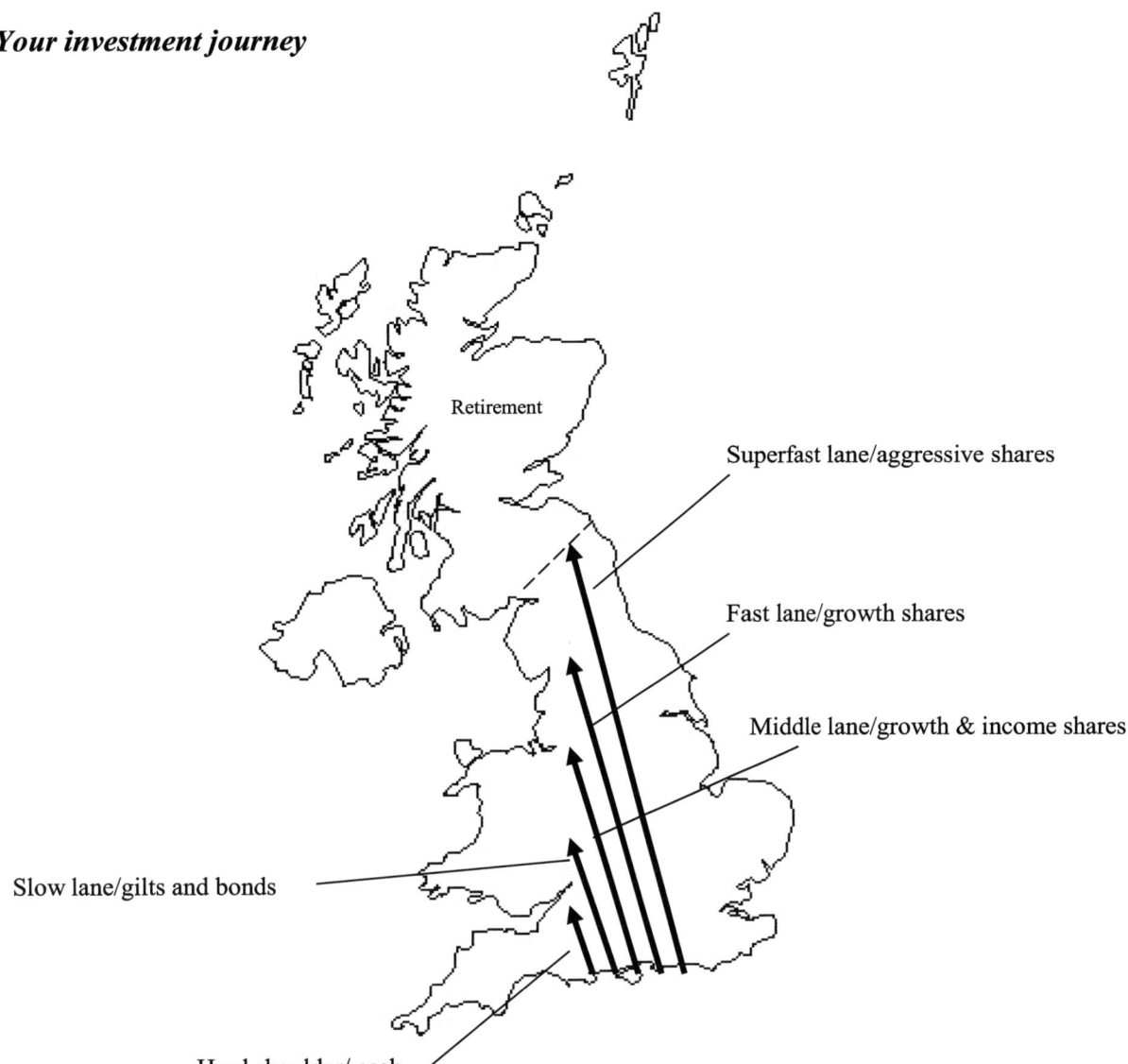

Retirement

Superfast lane/aggressive shares

Fast lane/growth shares

Middle lane/growth & income shares

Slow lane/gilts and bonds

Hard shoulder/ cash

Reducing your chance of an accident

There is a very simple rule you should follow when investing in the stock market and that is 'spend **time in** the market rather than **timing** the market'. What does this really mean? If you want to actively buy and sell shares all the time and try to 'time' it so you buy when the prices are low and sell again when they are high, you need to be prepared for losses. Unless you are particularly skilled at trading the markets, for the average and inexperienced investor, this is a sure fire way for you to make a loss.

When 'timing' the market by buying and selling constantly you can easily miss really good days of growth. It has been proven that even missing just 10 of the highest days' growth in the year can have a huge negative impact on the overall return you get at the end of the year. This also applies to people who worry when there is a drop in the market and go and take their money out and put it in a savings account until the market goes back up.

Think about what is being done here

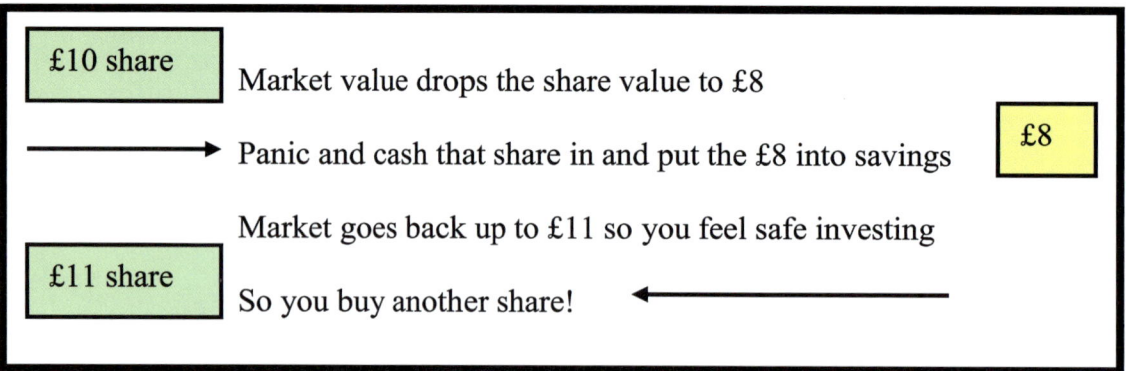

This is a very typical scenario for most inexperienced investors and by doing this not only have you crystallised a loss of £2 but you have also missed the growth of £1. If you just leave the money where it is, as long as you don't need it of course, give it time and it will be go back up again and the chances are you will see that bit of extra growth too.

A good thing to remember to help with this is: *Invest when you have the money and take it out when you need it.* That way you are not trying to time the market and instead you are spending time in it. The longer you spend in the market the better your return is likely to be.

Another key to reducing your risk is diversification. If you choose to have all your eggs in one basket, if something happens to that basket, it's a lot to lose. So by spreading your investments around you can significantly reduce this risk.

Firstly invest in all the different asset classes; Own and live in your house, invest in the stock and bond markets and have some savings in cash. That way you have a bit in cash, a bit in property, some in bonds and some in stocks. So if one type of investment has a wobble, your overall portfolio does not lose too much. The recent decline in the housing market, stock market, bond market and cash all in conjunction with each other was unprecedented, they do not normally react like this. It is of course unknown if this will be the case again but you should ask yourself why risk having all your money in one type of asset and rely on that assets performance when you can reap the benefits of many?

Diversification

There are many different industries represented within the stock market and the key to successful investing and reducing your risk is to make sure you have holdings in each one. Realistically if you are going to build a portfolio of individual share holdings, a good guideline for doing this effectively is to have a minimum of £100,000 to invest. Any less than this and you should really use pooled investments (discussed later) instead for your serious long term investing and set aside some 'play' money for stock market gambling. This way you can create an effective level of diversification across the different industries.

Each industry within the stock market reacts differently to different economic environments, so by having your money spread about you are reducing your overall risk.

The UK Stock Market (FTSE 100) Industry Sectors

Aerospace & Defence	Industrial Metals & Mining
Alternative Energy	Industrial Transportation
Banks	Leisure Goods
Beverages	Life Insurance
Chemicals	Media
Construction & Materials	Mining
Electricity	Mobile Telecommunications
Electronic & Electrical Equipment	Non-Equity Investment Instruments
Equity Investment Instruments	Non Life Insurance
Financial Services	Oil & Gas Producers
Fixed Line Telecommunications	Oil Equipment & Services
Food & Drug Retailers	Personal Goods
Food Producers	Pharmaceuticals & Biotechnology
Forestry & Paper	Real Estate Investment & Services
Gas, Water & Multi-utilities	Real Estate Investment Trusts
General Industries	Software & Computer Services
General Retailers	Support Services
Healthcare Equipment & Services	Technology Hardware & Equipment
Household Goods & Home Construction	Tobacco
Industrial Engineering	Travel & Leisure

More often than not portfolios of individual share holdings people have built up themselves will be overweight in a particular asset class, making the portfolio far riskier than they would consider themselves to be. There is also likely to be an overload of either utility or financial companies, with no holdings in any other industries. This can be the result of all the free shares that were given out when the utility companies went private or when banks have merged. If this is the case for you, then you should consider selling some off to repurchase other industries to reduce your risk.

Another thing people often do is say they are low risk investors and then go and purchase thousands of pounds of one particular share because a certain Sunday financial paper said it was a good idea! There are two things to consider here: (1) If you have read about it in the paper, the opportunity to make a quick buck will have long passed and (2) you have just put thousands with one company. What happens if that company then folds in a week's time? You will have lost all of your investment and as a result you would tell everyone that investing is a really bad idea because you lost all your money. If you really wanted to buy individual shares, the sensible option would be to split your investment amount down to at least four different holdings and then if one company goes bust, you have the other 3 to back you up.

Pooled investments

Pooled investments can be called many different things, according to the actual way the pooled investment works on a technical basis but generally they are known as;

- Unit trusts
- Mutual funds
- Open ended investment companies (OEICS)

Although pooled investments differ slightly with technicalities they have the same basic make up. They take lots of shares or bonds from different companies, pool them all together and then sell the customer either a unit of or a share in the overall investment. (All are commonly referred to as 'funds' no matter what type of pooled investment they are). Each fund is likely to hold from fourty to sixty different company's shares within it. This mass holding greatly reduces your risk as one company going to the wall will make a much smaller impact on the overall fund value (and therefore your capital holding) than if you held a single holding of shares in that company.

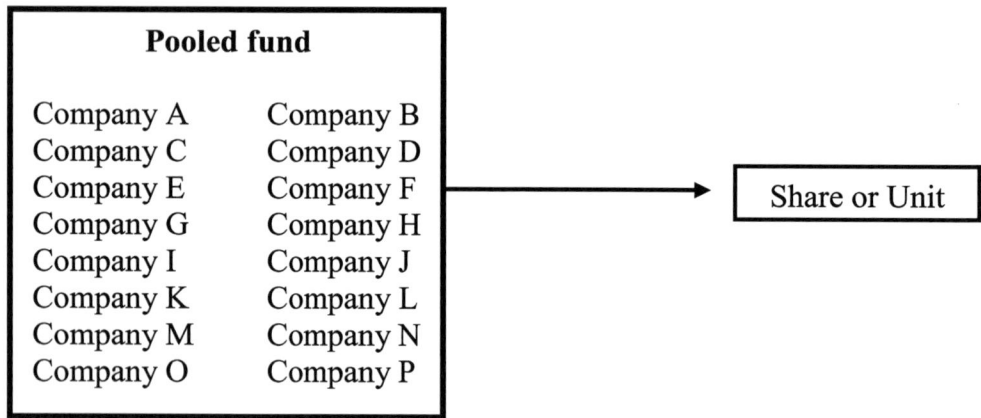

A good analogy for the reduction of risk offered by a pooled investment is this: imagine if you bought a table with four legs and one broke, you would not be able to use the table any more. If however you bought a table with thirty legs and one broke, you would hardly notice. This is the basic idea behind pooled investments. They enable you to diversify your funds way beyond that of an individual share portfolio. If you are worried that by investing you may lose all of your money, a pooled investment can virtually wipe that fear out. In order for you to lose all your money every single company held within the fund, in each of the different industries, would have to fold overnight for the fund manager to not have a chance of removing that company from the fund and replacing it with another. For this situation to happen across all the different industries in one night you would basically be looking at armageddon and if that was the case, I highly suspect worrying about your investments will be the last thing on your mind. So unlike individual share holdings where yes, you can potentially lose all your money, pooled investments help to avoid this.

Another benefit of a pooled investment is the companies held within it are not just there because they look like they are doing well but (with most reputable funds) they will be there because they have a met a very strict investing criterion or the analysts for that fund know the company inside out. They will have studied the business's strategies in order to know how they work so they can decide from the inside looking out, whether or not it is a good investment. This is something you simply cannot achieve from an individual share holder's perspective.

By knowing the businesses inside the investment so well or by having a very strict criterion for entry, it also means that the fund manager is able to pull investments out before they go bad and replace them with ones that are doing better.

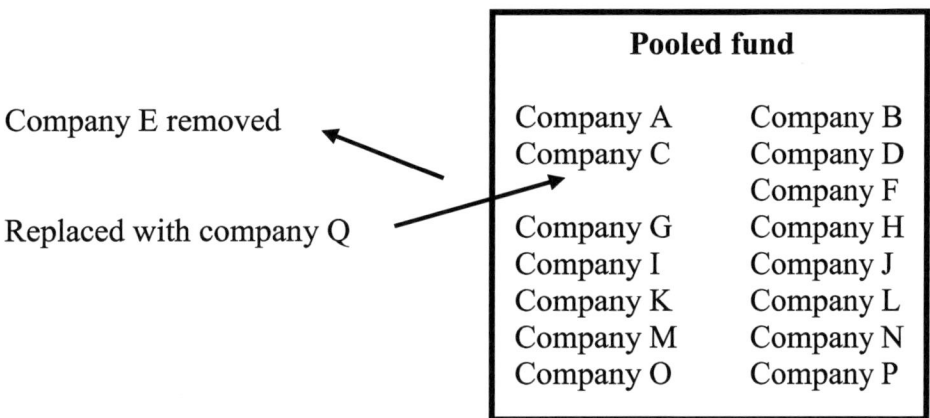

Diversification with funds
Funds can offer diversification in many different formats (in addition to holding lots of company's shares in one pot). The most common funds specialise is one particular asset class ie growth and income shares and then within that they hold fourty to sixty different company's growth and income shares, all spread from across the eight industries on the stock market.

Alternatively, they can specialise in a particular industry ie technologies or utilities and the fund will be made of lots of different companies' shares from within that industry but spread across the different asset classes.

Finally, they can also specialise in different geographical regions, either spread across the different asset classes or in just one.

Types of funds
Gilt Funds
Corporate bond funds
Fixed interest funds (containing corporate bonds and gilts)
Income funds (gilts, corporate bonds, growth & income shares either mixed or specific)
Growth and income funds – often called high yield funds
Growth funds
Smaller companies funds
Specialist funds

Property funds
Multi asset funds
Tracker funds*

Geographical splits of funds
UK based funds
European including UK
European excluding UK
Asia including Japan
Asia excluding Japan
North America
Emerging markets
Japan
Global

Tracker Funds
A tracker fund is one which tracks a particular market, so for example in the UK it may track the FTSE 100 or in the USA it may track the Dow Jones (their stock market). With this type of fund you need to be aware that it is not actively managed by a fund manager on your behalf. Your investment will do exactly what the stock market does, hence the name tracker. This is great in a rising market but not so good in a falling one when you need a good fund manager to reduce the losses by actively buying and selling holdings on your behalf.

Building a portfolio
If you choose to build a portfolio of investments using pooled funds instead of individual shares, you will still need to ensure that you diversify across the different asset classes (bonds, growth & income shares, growth shares etc) according to your personal risk preference.

You should also consider investing in some funds outside of the UK.

International investing
Many do not want to invest in any country other than the UK because they think it is too risky; however it is possible that you are increasing your risk by limiting yourself to just one country. In the old days you could rest assured that if the UK was having financial problems this did not mean that Europe, North America or Asia would be too. (Of course this has all changed since the global recession we have recently experienced). However there is still a strong argument for investing some of your money internationally rather than keeping it all in the UK, when it comes to reducing your risk and diversifying.

Have a think about the biggest brand names you know, Coca Cola Enterprises, Microsoft and Apple to name but a few. These are all internationally based companies, so if you do not invest in either a global fund or one that specialises in their industries you would not get access to these big companies and their even bigger profits.

By limiting yourself to just the UK you are reducing the potential return that your portfolio can provide you with and also increasing your risk. You don't need to have lots held abroad and don't overweigh yourself with these if you are a cautious investor but make sure you have some.

Something to be mindful of when you are investing internationally is the effect of the exchange rate on the value of your investment when you come to cash it in. The fund details will indicate if returns are shown after they have been converted to GBP or not.

Purchasing a Portfolio

To help ease any confusion, it is necessary to explain the difference between purchasing a portfolio and building one.

If you go to see either a stock broker or an independent financial adviser then you will need to **build** a portfolio according to your risk tolerance. This means buying a variety of different funds (or shares) spread across the different asset classes to give you an overall portfolio that is either designed to grow or to produce an income (or a mix of both) in line with your risk profile. By doing it this way, you will have access to a variety of providers.

The alternative to this is if you go to see an adviser at the bank or building society, there you can **purchase** a set portfolio (bit like purchasing a set meal) that matches your risk profile. For example; you take the risk test and this tells them you are a medium risk investor, they will provide you with their medium risk portfolio. It will likely have in it a bond fund, a growth and income fund, a growth fund and probably some international shares for good measure. You will not need to concern yourself with what amount of which fund to buy, it is all set out for you already. All you need to do is decide how much of your money you would like to invest.

Purchasing a set portfolio can be the best solution if you are an inexperienced and cautious investor because it is the most straightforward process of all. However, it can be very limiting and you are potentially reducing your return because all the funds held within your portfolio are pre determined by the provider and are not necessarily chosen because they are the best performing ones on the market. (Please note; at most banks and building societies you are also able to select your own funds from a set list of those provided if you request to do so).

Another point to note here is the risk ratings for banks/building societies and brokers and IFA's. Banks and building society set portfolios are far less risky than their counterparts within the industry. For example; a medium risk portfolio with the bank will be about the same risk level as a low risk portfolio anywhere else. As they are such large institutions they need to be overly cautious with the level of risk they expose you to. This can be a benefit if you are a cautious investor but not if you are someone who wants to get to your destination quickly!

Should you decide that you would like to purchase your own investments without the assistance of a professional, whether that be a broker, banker or independent financial adviser then there are numerous websites that you can use for this. You will have a choice of building your own portfolio or you can purchase a set risk portfolio, like those available at the bank.

Tied Agents
Be cautious of tied agents. These are companies that can only sell one providers' investments because they are 'tied' in an agreement with them. This is most likely the case with banks and building societies but can also apply to other financial advisers as well. If this is the case, I recommend you research the products from that provider first to ensure you are happy with the return they give in comparison to similar funds on the market.

How to tell a good fund
One of the best ways to tell a good fund manager is not the growth they have made in an up market, as most would believe but in fact the losses in a down market.

Anyone can make a profit in a bull (rising) market because prices are going up but what you need is a good fund manager who will make the right buy and sell decisions in a bear (falling) market thus reducing the overall losses the fund experiences.

There have been two substantial drops in the market in the last 10 years that will enable you to check out these figures. In 2001 – 2002 the stock market dropped 50% in value; in 2007 – 2008 it dropped 30%. A not so good fund will be one that dropped either the full amount or more and a very good fund will be one that dropped only half of this amount and anything else in between should be judged accordingly.

When you are comparing similar funds to each other, it is a good idea to check out the overall rating in their specific category. If they are the number 1 fund of that type, how long have they held that spot for? Have they been in the top twenty for the last 5+ years? It is worth considering those funds that have been consistently good performers year on year in comparison to ad hoc top performers.

Managing your portfolio
If you are paying a professional to manage your portfolio for you, then they will guide you on buying and selling decisions to get the best return and reduce the losses you experience with your investment. Be cautious of the adviser who recommends you sell and repurchase too often as this is known as 'churning' and is illegal because they are making profits each time they purchase investments on your behalf.

A guideline to follow is to not sell an investment based on performance unless you have held it for at least five years. This gives it a typical five year stock market cycle to perform and if it hasn't by then you can consider getting rid of it and buying something else. (Please note that this is only a guideline and each investment should be looked at on an individual basis).

Tax is not covered in much detail in this book but for the benefit of those with large sums of investments, it is important to manage your portfolio to reduce your capital gains tax liability. This is often an area that is somewhat ignored or forgotten unless you have a very good adviser.

Tax

Capital Gains Tax is a charge put on the profit you make on the sale of certain assets, such as shares, investment property, antiques etc. Each year the Government allocates a Capital Gains Tax allowance for each individual and you are able to make a profit up to this amount without receiving any tax charge. Any amount above this will be liable to tax. The allowance for this tax year is £10,600 and the new tax charges are 18% and 28% per cent tax rates for individuals (the tax rate used depends on the total amount of taxable income but can basically be seen as basic and higher rate taxpayers).

For any shares not held within an investment ISA, every year you should sell a large enough holding of your investments (that you have seen growth on) to use up your Capital Gains Tax allowance and then repurchase them. This ensures that you keep the same level of investments but have reduced the growth, as far as the tax man is concerned. Instead of leaving it 20 years and when you need to sell them receiving a huge Capital Gains Tax bill for all the profit that you have made over that time. (gilts and corporate bonds are not liable to Capital Gains Tax).

The income produced from gilts and corporate bonds (if not held within a tax efficient product) is liable to Income Tax at your personal rate. This is not taken at source like savings accounts and must be paid via your tax return.

The dividend produced from growth and income shares, has an automatic 10% tax charge made on it, this is taken at source. This 10% cannot be shielded by any tax efficient product and if you are a basic rate or non-taxpayer it remains at this level. If however you are a higher rate taxpayer the charge increases to 32.5% and if you are an additional rate tax payer the charge is 42.5% (these higher charges are paid via your tax return and not taken at source). It should be noted here that although this is high, for a higher rate taxpayer it is still lower than the 40% you would be charged on any cash savings, so therefore making shares an effective tax tool for some.

Tax efficient products

There are a variety of different products for you to hold your investments in. You do not have to hold investments in a product but there are various tax advantages available if you choose to do so.

The main products available to help reduce your tax are; Investment ISAs, Pensions and Capital Investment Bonds. Please note that banks and building societies will often give their own names to capital investment bonds as well as providing other products for you to hold your investments in that are taxable. You will need to check with your provider to establish what you have.

In the fridge section of this book ISAs were referred to as being buckets. For ease of understanding consider all the products discussed here as being buckets that you can carry your investments in, with each bucket providing different benefits.

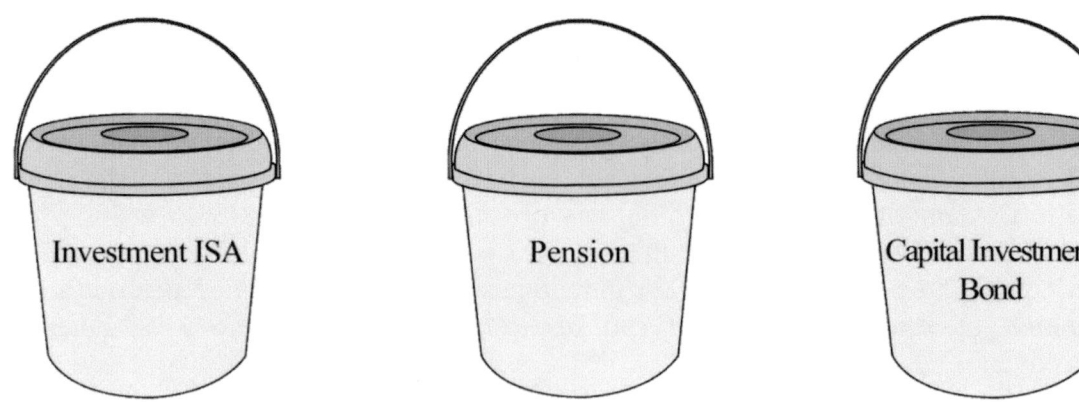

Investment ISA's

As previously discussed your ISA bucket has a capacity of £11,280 for this current tax year and this can be split between cash and investments. The bucket will protect you from paying Income Tax on your interest and Capital Gains Tax on your growth. You can invest any amount up to the full £11,280, according to what you put in your cash ISA. You have to be 18 years old to invest in an investment ISA of your own (16 years for cash) and you can continue to invest until you die.

You can add money to an investment ISA either as a regular amount each month, as one lump sum or in ad hoc amounts, as long as you do not exceed the maximum allowance for the tax year. You can also take funds out of your ISA easily and there should not be any penalty for doing this, please check this with your own provider. (Remember that it can take up to 10 days for any investment you hold to give you funds back as the investments need to be sold on the stock market first and processed before the money filters through to you.) You can hold an ISA for as long as you want and you can also take money out in any form that you want, either as lump sums or a tax efficient income.

Inside your investment ISA you can hold individual shares, corporate bonds and pooled investments. Any growth you see within the ISA stays within it and is protected from Income Tax and Capital Gains Tax. As with your cash ISA you are able to pick your bucket up and move it to another provider (must be done by transfer not you) but you can also change the investments held within that ISA if they are not performing to your liking.

People often say 'My ISA is not performing' or 'I don't want any more ISAs the one I have is doing really badly'. To this you should consider the following; If you have a really bad cup of coffee at a restaurant, do you blame the coffee or the cup? Of course the answer is the coffee. Now apply this to your ISA, it is not the ISA that is performing badly but the investments you have chosen to hold inside it. All the ISA is doing is providing a bucket for you to hold those investments in and stopping tax from leaking out. If you are not happy with how it is performing, change what is inside it.

Pensions

Unfortunately pensions have now got a really bad reputation. A reputation they don't necessarily deserve and as such, many people are now missing out on a great opportunity to protect their money from tax. The main reason for this bad reputation is that in his position as Chancellor Mr Brown decided, in his infinite wisdom, that he was going to put the 10% tax credit charge on dividends and that no tax efficient investment product could protect investors from this charge. As I am sure you can imagine pensions hold huge sums of money, with a large proportion of it in growth and income shares. The dividends from these shares play a major role in the overall growth of the investment, by taking 10% off every single dividend payment that is made within the fund – the overall effect is a very substantial loss. It was this single move that wiped huge amounts off the value of every single pension fund in the country, along side affecting the growth of every investor's portfolio.

Add this to a downturn in the market and a good dose of the media and you have cooked up a storm. Pensions are the one type of investment that everybody recognises the name of so when the media want to report losses in the stock market the easiest way for them to do this is to refer to pensions. The end result is everybody hating them, when plain and simply they are just another tax efficient investment product.

What does a pension do?
So what does a pension actually do? Like an ISA it protects your money from tax. Unlike an ISA you can have a pension from birth, so if you wanted to start a pension for a new born then you could do so. When you put money into a pension the Government give you your tax back at whatever is your highest rate (if you do not pay tax at all 20% is still added). The investments inside the pension then grow free from capital gains and income tax. The big difference between an ISA and a pension though is taking your money back out.

Taking money out of a pension
With a pension you are not allowed to take any money out until you have retired, the lowest age you can access it is 55yrs. When you take money out, you are allowed 25% of the total fund value as a lump sum. (There is no tax charge on this 25% so it is referred to as a tax free cash lump sum). The remaining 75% can be used to buy an income for life, otherwise known as an annuity or it can be re-invested to create an income, however it is recommended that you have a minimum of £100,000 to invest before you consider this option. The only time you are allowed to have the whole of your pension fund as one cash sum is if the total sum of all of your pension pots together at retirement come to less than £18,000.

Putting money in a pension.
As with an ISA there is a limit on how much money you can make tax efficient. The maximum you are allowed to put into a pension in one year is a capped maximum, of £50,000. If you do not work then the maximum you can put in is £3600. It is important to note here that the amount you can personally put in must be the total less the tax the Government will add. So for example; If you do not work you can contribute £2880 the Government will then add the 20% to bring the total up to £3600. What other investment would you see 20% instant growth on your money such as this? This fact in itself should make a pension something worth considering. Not forgetting of course that if you have a work pension, your employer may also add money in for you too.

A big difference between ISAs and pensions is how many you are allowed to have in one year. As previously explained you are only allowed one Investment ISA a year with one provider. With your pension however, you can contribute to as many as you like as long as you do not exceed your total salary for that year, (this amount is capped). So you could have a pension with your employer and then hold various private pensions in addition to this.

When you leave an employer, your pension with them will either be frozen or you may be able to transfer it into either your new employer's pension or a private pension. If you choose to leave it frozen where it is, be hot on your paperwork. There are likely to be a good number of years between now and when you retire, with a lot of house moves. Make sure you stay in contact with the pension provider so that you always have up to date details. It may not amount to much but once you retire you will want every bit of money owed to you.

A standard pension will hold pooled investments. When you set your pension up you will either be given the chance to choose these or they will be chosen for you based on your risk tolerance. If you would like to hold individual shares or bonds inside your pension then you will need to have a SIPP – Self Invested Personal Pension but in order to have one of these you will need to be able to invest reasonably large sums of money.

Just like your ISA, if your pension is not performing then you can change what is inside it and you can also change providers. The one thing to be cautious of with pensions is provider's charges. Quite often these can be really high and if you only have a small amount of money in your pension charges can have a very detrimental impact on the overall value of it. If charges are high you may sometimes see no growth at all because the charges eat into it all. Keep an eye on this and shop around for a better provider with cheaper charges.

If you go and see a professional they will likely offer you a free analysis service because they would like you to move your pension to them. This is a great idea to take up because they have to provide you with a forecast of the growth they could offer you in comparison to your current provider (meaning they do all the leg work and you simply make the decision). Not many people take this opportunity up and choose to leave their pension sitting there rotting instead, Continuing to add a good percentage of their monthly income to it and then wonder why it's not worth anything when they get to retirement.

Think about your journey, when would you like to get to your destination? What would you like to do when you get there? Actively manage what lane you want your pension to be in for its journey to retirement so that you can have the biggest amount to spend possible once you are there. Aside from a house, a pension is likely to be the biggest investment most will make in their lives, so manage it to its best advantage!

Putting money into a pension

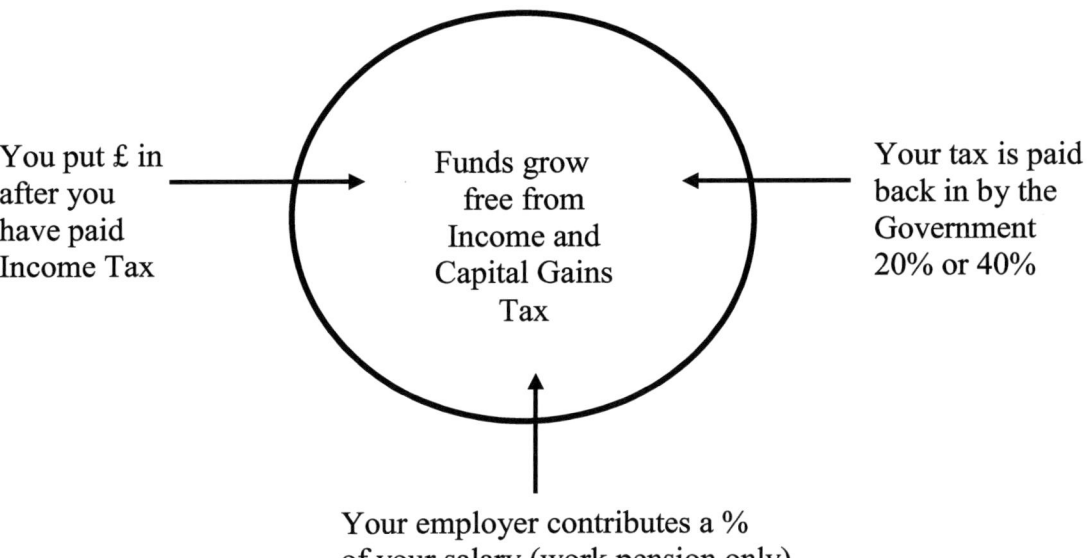

You put £ in after you have paid Income Tax

Funds grow free from Income and Capital Gains Tax

Your tax is paid back in by the Government 20% or 40%

Your employer contributes a % of your salary (work pension only)

Putting money into an ISA

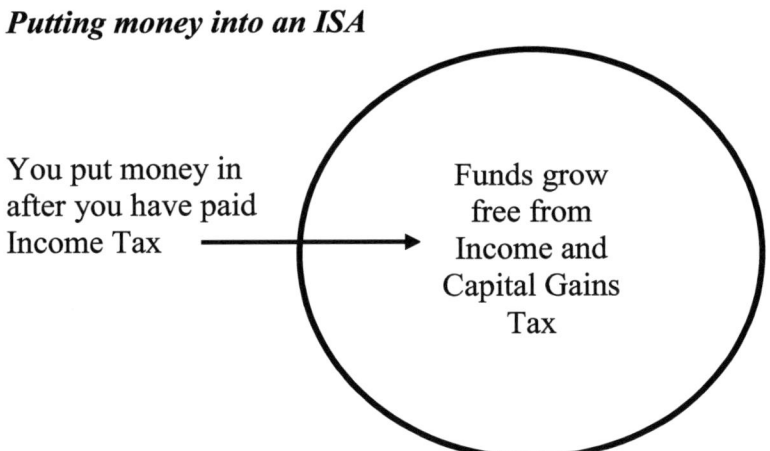

You put money in after you have paid Income Tax

Funds grow free from Income and Capital Gains Tax

Taking money out of a pension (at retirement)

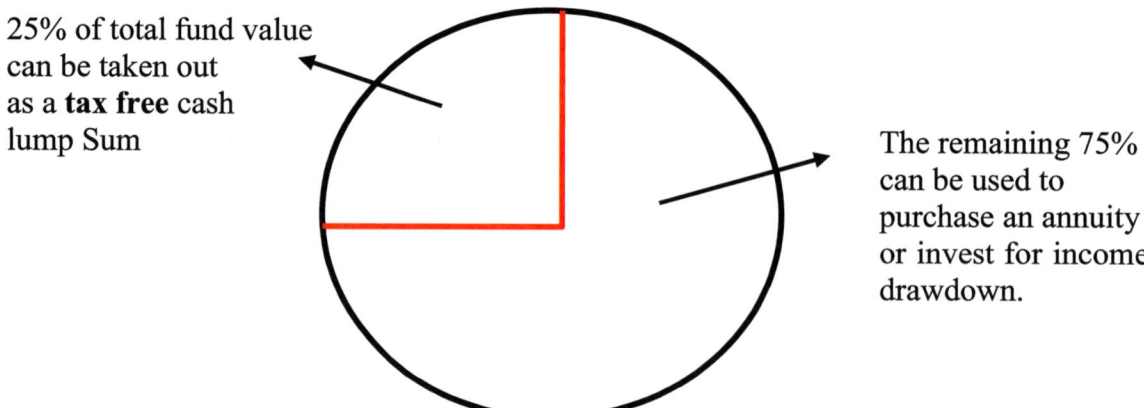

25% of total fund value can be taken out as a **tax free** cash lump Sum

The remaining 75% can be used to purchase an annuity or invest for income drawdown.

Please note: You do not have to take 25% out as a tax free cash lump sum, you can take any amount up to this, or you can use the full 100% of fund value to purchase your annuity. However, because you will pay tax on the income produced from the annuity it is worth considering having the full amount of tax free cash out so that you can choose what you do with it. (see section on producing an income in retirement).

Taking money out of an ISA (any age)

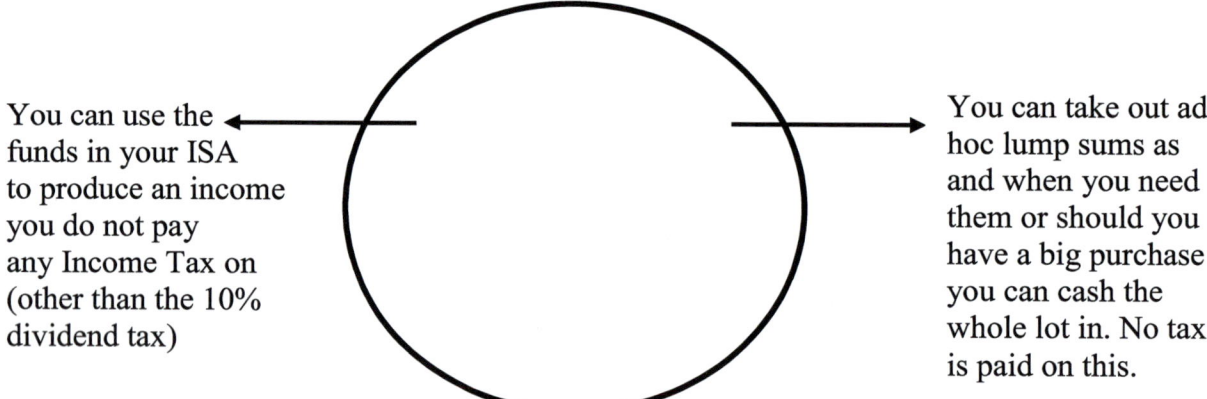

You can use the funds in your ISA to produce an income you do not pay any Income Tax on (other than the 10% dividend tax)

You can take out ad hoc lump sums as and when you need them or should you have a big purchase you can cash the whole lot in. No tax is paid on this.

ISA versus pension when saving for retirement

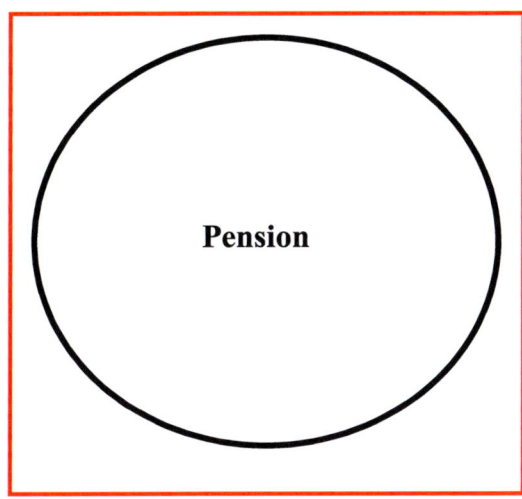

Limited access

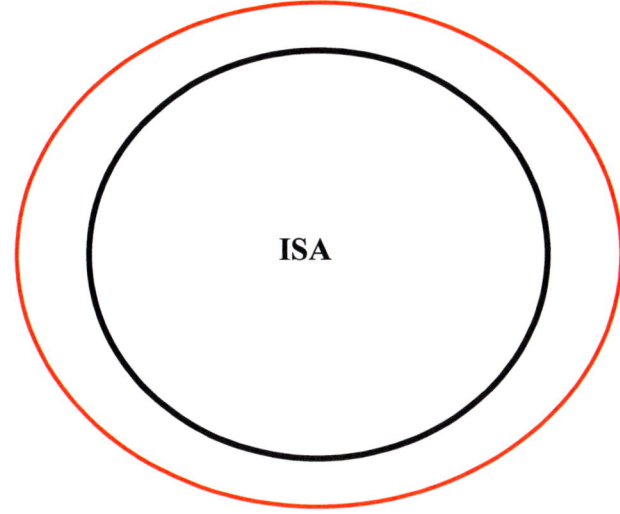

Easy access

Both offer different tax protection and therefore in an ideal situation you should consider having both types of products in your portfolio. A good example of this would be to have a work pension (so you can take full advantage of both your employer and the Government adding money to your pot) but also have an ISA each year to independently build up your own funds giving you a pot that is accessible any time in your life should you need it.

Pension	**Investment ISA**
<ul><li>Any amount up to your annual salary capped or £3600 if not working.</li><li>Tax added back in at start</li><li>Tax paid on income taken out</li><li>Grows free of Income Tax and Capital Gains Tax</li><li>25% tax free cash lump</li><li>Can only access at retirement</li><li>Invest from birth</li><li>Max age 75</li><li>Must convert to income by 75</li><li>Can hold pooled investments</li><li>Can change products held within</li><li>Can transfer to different provider</li></ul>	<ul><li>£11,280 maximum, less if Cash ISA allowance used.</li><li>Contributions made after tax</li><li>No tax to pay on income (except 10% tax on dividends)</li><li>Grows free of Income Tax and Capital Gains Tax</li><li>No tax or limit on lump sums</li><li>Access at any time</li><li>Minimum age 18years</li><li>No maximum age</li><li>No limits on use</li><li>Can hold any investments</li><li>Can change products held within</li><li>Can transfer to different provider</li></ul>

Cash

A small word needs to be said regarding saving towards retirement just in cash. Should you choose to do this, consider the motorway described earlier and have another look at where the hard shoulder option will get you on the journey. It is basically like choosing to drive on to the motorway and then get out and push your car up the hard shoulder. From the South coast, it's going to take you more than a lifetime to ever reach the Scottish border, you need to drive there.

Property

Property is of course another option as a retirement plan that a lot of people use. Before the mortgage crash this was a reasonably good idea because anyone was able to get a 100% mortgage and then rent the property out to pay the mortgage payments, giving you the asset of an additional property by the time you retire. The downfall of this method has already been seen. However another important point to consider here is tax.

If you purchase a property as your investment vehicle for retirement, at a young age and that property grows at least 50% in value over your lifetime, should you choose to sell it once you are retired that will be an awful lot of your profit that you are losing to capital gains tax. Not only this, but property is not a liquid investment so should you need any money during your life, you can't exactly sell the bathroom. Not forgetting of course the ongoing costs involved in the upkeep of the property, months when you do not have a tenant paying the mortgage etc. Although a property may seem like the easy and most understandable option, it is actually a costly and limiting retirement plan to undertake.

Capital investment bonds

A capital investment bond is the last of the tax efficient buckets. It is a product that lends itself more to creating an income in retirement than saving for it because you cannot save regularly into it. However if you have a lump sum and you have used your ISA then it should also be considered as a beneficial product used to protect your growth from Capital Gains Tax.

You are able to hold different pooled investments inside the bond and you can either choose these from a list supplied by the provider or you can determine the level of risk you wish to take and the funds will be automatically selected for you, (much similar to purchasing a portfolio in accordance to your risk level).

In addition to your investments, a capital investment bond will also have an element of life insurance attached to it. It is important to remember that this policy is of no significance to you as actual life insurance because it will only ever cover what you have invested. You therefore need to ensure that you also have a sufficient amount of life cover, held by a separate and specific life insurance policy. The life insurance policy is used to give the product certain tax advantages that other products do not have.

Paying money in

There is usually a minimum amount you can invest in to a capital investment bond set by the provider, in the region of £3000. The upper limit for one bond is usually about £500,000. This can differ per provider and is not a Government set maximum. You can hold as many bonds as you want, with the same or different providers and there are no limits to how many you can invest in, in any one year. The provider will usually allow you to make ad hoc additional contributions to the bond but is likely to be a minimum amount for this. One thing you cannot do however is make regular contributions to it, due to the way it is viewed by the taxman. There is usually an upper age limit that you can contribute to a bond (this can differ per provider). The lowest age for contributions is 18years, as with all investments.

Taking money out

Any growth within a capital investment bond is free of Capital Gains Tax. The bond pays Corporation Tax at a rate of 28% and this is considered sufficient, so there is no further tax to pay for the basic rate taxpayer. A disadvantage of this bond is if you are a non taxpayer you cannot claim back the 28%.

Money can be withdrawn either as an income or a lump sum. The maximum amount you are allowed to withdraw without any further tax is 5% per annum. This is an accumulative amount so if you do not use the allowance for three years, in the third year you would be able to withdraw 15% as a lump sum without any tax liability. The percentage is based on your initial investment amount, not the fund value at the time of withdrawal.

If you were wishing to take a regular income from the bond then this would be 5%, paid either monthly, quarterly, half yearly or annually. Should you need to have a larger withdrawal than this, the maximum is 7.5% but you could incur an income tax charge for this depending on your personal tax status. These bonds are a beneficial way of producing a planned income in retirement, although it should be noted that the income will not increase in line with inflation.

Cashing your bond in

Most bonds have a five year minimum investment term, which you will need to hold the bond for before you are able to cash it in. Cashing it in prior to this is likely to incur high charges.

When you cash the bond in, the growth that it has produced is considered as income and is added to your annual income for that tax year. There is no further tax to pay if your annual income (including the bond's growth) remains within the basic rate tax bracket. If however it pushes you into the higher rate taxpayer's bracket, there will be a tax liability and this is taxed as income tax. However, there is a method known as top slicing which is applied to this calculation, dividing the growth of the bond by the years of investment and this decreases the level of income tax liability. If this applies to you, seek assistance from a tax or investment adviser prior to cashing in to ensure you have the correct strategy in place to maximise the benefit of this type of bond.

Regular saving

Chances are during your working life the only type of saving you can do is a regular amount from your salary each month. If you have a work pension then you will have a regular monthly amount coming out of your wages and going automatically into your pension. Question is though, what are you doing with the rest? If you are saving into cash you should consider saving into the stock market instead. If you decide to do this you must first make sure that you have a contingency fund in place and any planned spending is saved separately. (So that you do not have to dip into your investments and can instead leave them to grow).

The good news is that saving monthly into the stock market is pretty much the most effective way you can do it and over time will give you potentially a much larger return than investing the same amount as a lump sum. This is known as pound cost averaging.

Pound cost averaging

This is the name given to investing a regular amount into an investment at regular intervals, usually done as a set amount every month. The investment will either be individual shares or pooled investments.

By investing on a regular basis you are able to smooth out the fluctuations experienced in the stock market. Some months when you buy the market will be high and other months it will be low. When you are investing on a regular basis it is beneficial for you if the stock market is quite volatile, as this gives you more drops to take advantage of. You therefore may want to consider investing in a higher risk profile than you would consider yourself to be to take full advantage of this.

Investing regularly also takes a lot of the worry out of investing because you do not have to worry whether you are investing at a peak or not. There will be peaks and troughs continuously over the months that you invest. (Please note the figures given below are examples only).

Investing a lump sum

End of the Year

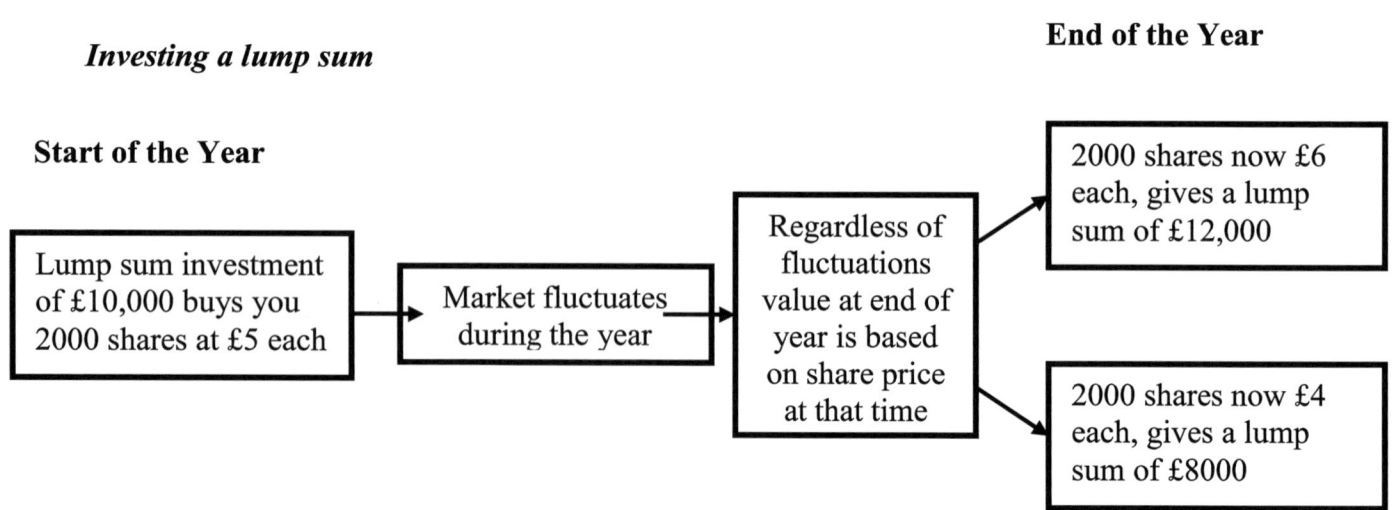

£10,000 split into 12 monthly payments of £833

Jan	Feb	Mar	Apr	May	June	July	Aug	Sep	Oct	Nov	Dec
£833	£833	£833	£833	£833	£833	£833	£833	£833	£833	£833	£833
Shares at £5 each	Market up shares £5.50 each	Market up shares £6.00 each	Market down shares £5.75 each	Market down shares £5.50 each	Market down shares £4.75 each	Market down shares £4.00 each	Market up shares £4.15 each	Market up shares £4.35 each	Market down shares £4.20 each	Market up shares £4.75 each	Market up shares £5.50 each
Total	Total	Total	Total	Total	Total	Total	Total	Total	Total	Total	Total
166 shares	151 shares	138 shares	144 shares	151 shares	175 shares	208 shares	200 shares	191 shares	198 shares	175 shares	151 shares

> Total shares at end of year 2048

You can see the from the example above, by investing on a monthly basis, due to the fluctuations you have an extra 48 shares in comparison to investing as a lump sum, where your have a static amount. The additional shares bought when the market is down can almost be considered as free shares because you will make pure profit on these when the market goes back up, creating a win/win situation by investing regularly.

Turning the stock market into a win/win situation

High market (win one)

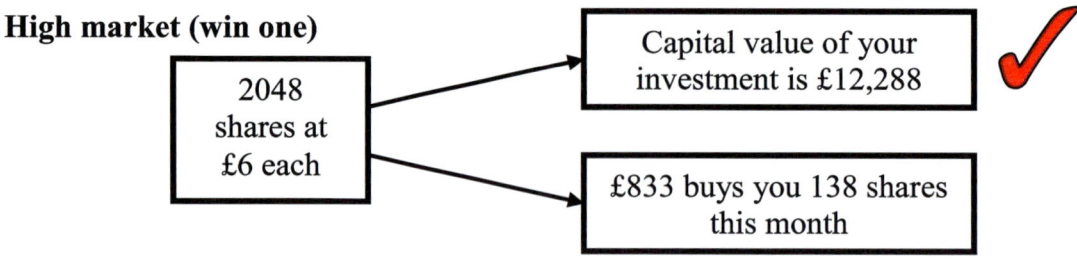

Low market (win two)

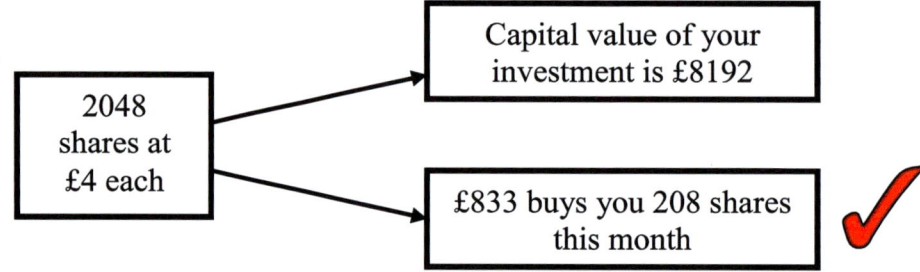

In a low market you can see that although your capital value is worth less, this month you are getting seventy more shares than you did when the market was high, so when the market goes back up to £6 again those seventy shares alone have made you an extra £420.

Cash
If you are currently doing a regular saver into a cash account, think of the comparison here. If you were saving the same £833, each month that would earn you the same flat amount of interest, let's say a generous 7% and compare that at the end of the year.

Jan	Feb	Mar	Apr	May	June	July	Aug	Sep	Oct	Nov	Dec
£833	£833	£833	£833	£833	£833	£833	£833	£833	£833	£833	£833
7%	7%	7%	7%	7%	7%	7%	7%	7%	7%	7%	7%
£58.31	£58.31	£58.31	£58.31	£58.31	£58.31	£58.31	£58.31	£58.31	£58.31	£58.31	£58.31

Total at end of year £10,699.72

Although this is potentially higher than if there was a down market as illustrated above, you would manage your own finances in this situation and simply not cash your investments in at this time. Instead, having seen the extra you can make, you would continue to invest, taking advantage of being able to purchase them at the lower price. This gives you the chance to far outgrow your return in the long run and continue to experience a win/win situation.

Summary of the freezer

- If you want to get more out of your money than simply saving it in cash and you are able to leave it for longer than a five year period then you should definitely consider putting it into your freezer/investments.

- There are lots of different asset types to choose from and you do not have to take lots of risk in order to get a better return than cash. The level of risk associated with different types of investments can be compared to the different lanes on the M25. How much risk you take will determine what level of growth you will see on your money in the longer term.

- Diversification is the key to successful investing and pooled investments can be used to do this effectively with a smaller amount of money than what is needed for an individual share portfolio.

- Your investments can be held in a variety of different products to make them tax efficient (ISA's, pensions and capital investment bonds) and these can be used to produce either growth, income or both.

- Regular saving is the most effective way to save into the stock market and creates a win/win situation when the market experiences any drops, giving you the potential for a greater return in the long run than a lump sum investment but without the stress.

- When saving for retirement, you need to consider either property or investments; cash alone is not effective enough. If you choose investments then you need to take advantage of the different tax efficient products available.

5

Taking money out of your fridge and freezer
(Hierarchy of accounts)

It is of course completely up to you what accounts you choose to take money from when you need it. However a good order to follow is this:

Taxable cash

Tax efficient cash

Taxable investments

Tax efficient investments

You should consider taking money from taxable cash first because once you take money out of your ISA you cannot put it back and therefore that tax efficient bucket is lost. Don't just take it out of the ISA because you feel it is not performing. Remember what was said before: change it, don't throw it away.

It is better to use money from your cash savings first because your investments are going to continue to work for you over the much longer term and will potentially give you a higher return than your cash. Consider your kitchen - would you take a steak out of the freezer to defrost and eat, if you have already had one in the fridge? However, it must be noted here that you should never leave yourself in a position where all of your assets are tied up in investments. Always ensure that you have at least your contingency fund available in easy to access cash.

When you do come to need access to your freezer investments, take what you need from any investments that you pay tax on, before your tax efficient ones. This is particularly relevant when it comes to taking money out of your investment ISA, for exactly the same reasons as stated above.

Don't forget that there are numerous tax efficient products you can hold investments in and these can all offer different benefits. If you are a higher rate tax payer then you should consider discussing with a tax adviser whether it is more beneficial for you to take money from your capital investment bonds or ISAs first as both can offer very different tax strategies. Also if you are using one investment for growth and one for income, it would obviously make sense to take money from your growth investments as a lump sum withdrawal because otherwise you may affect your income.

A note to mention here is pensions and the tax free cash lump sum you can take when you retire. Although pensions are also a tax efficient product whilst they are growing, once you start to take an income from them you will be taxed on that income. It therefore makes sense to take the tax free cash lump sum out of this investment when you can.

6

Creating an income in retirement

You have worked hard for your money all of your working life and now it is time for that money to work equally hard for you. A common trap that people fall in to when they retire is to stop seeing any long term needs for their finances but the chances are if you retire at sixty five you could well live at least another thirty years. If you do not manage your finances correctly when you first retire you could create a situation where you either have very little left or the value of what you have has decreased so dramatically with inflation, in real terms it is only worth half its value.

The attitude of many is that they don't mind this, the state will look after them but it should be considered, with great thought, whether you would really like to be in a position of financial insecurity at the most vulnerable time of your life? By planning correctly and continuing to take a longer term view of your finances you can not only create an income that will replenish your larder but also ensure that what is in your fridge and freezer continues to grow. Your choices are; Property, Cash and Investments.

Property

People like property as an investment because you can see, touch and manage it yourself and this makes them feel safe and secure. The benefit of purchasing a second property to create your income when you retire is that the income can increase with inflation because you are in control of how much you charge. There is also the additional benefit that the value of your capital investment will potentially grow over time, giving you the chance to get back more than you originally invested. However, there are disadvantages that should be considered.

A house is not liquid assets.
If you are considering using most of your available funds to purchase a second property when you retire, then you first need to determine what you will do if in 10yrs time you have a financial emergency and need to access some of your money? It is very hard to liquidate cash from an investment property – are you going to sell the bathroom? If you need cash then you would have to consider selling the property to free up what is needed. Not only will this take time (maybe more time than you have before you need the funds) but it will also cost you to do so. If the property market has fallen (as so many people experienced in recent years) you may get back less than you paid. If however it is worth more then you will potentially have to pay capital gains tax on your profit – this often takes most property investors by surprise. (Only applies to investment properties not your home) Unlike investments that you can wrap up in various products to protect from such taxes, there isn't any way of protecting property. On top of this cost you will also have the solicitors and estate agent fees.

Your income is not guaranteed

You may well find that property on a like for like comparison with some investments can produce you a greater monthly income but here are some events that could impact on this:

- Demand for rental properties in the area falls
- You don't get a tenant for a few months in a row
- A tenant turns into a squatter (and you can't get income from them or anyone else - not to mention the legal costs of having them removed).

Having a constant and regular income in retirement is essential to most people and if you are considering using property to create this then you must also have a large contingency buffer in place to support you if any of the above were to happen.

Ongoing costs

Another area that many fail to consider is the ongoing maintenance costs of property. Unfortunately most tenants do not treat a property with quite the same respect as you do your home and this can lead to many costly problems, either on an on going basis if they report every little thing to you or a big bill if they don't bother and the little problems turn into big ones. Either way, when you take out the ongoing cost of maintenance from the monthly income, you will more than likely find that it drops quite considerably. Again, if you choose this option for retirement you need to make sure that you have a suitable contingency fund and savings.

Inheritance Tax

Unfortunately there is very little that can be done to protect property assets from Inheritance Tax. If this is not planned for in advance, families receiving a house of greater value than the nil rate band can face a difficult financial situation, as the property and other assets are not released from probate until the Inheritance Tax bill has been paid.

Long Term Care

Long Term Care is another area where it is not beneficial to have property as your assets because the state will sell it to pay for the care. However there are investments available that can protect against this (at the same time as protecting against Inheritance Tax), helping to keep funds within your family. However moving your money into such investments cannot be done at the last minute when you find you have to go into care. You will need to have held such investments for a considerable time prior to this, (a minimum of one year). Otherwise it can be seen as intentional degradation of assets and the state can still liquidise them to pay for your care. Even if you are just retiring, this type of longer term planning is worth considering.

Cash

The biggest benefit of cash is having a stable capital value. Unlike property and investments that fluctuate, whatever you have in cash (as long as you don't spend it) remains the same. For many who are going into the uncertain times of retirement, with little or no income, having this solid amount in cash provides the sense of stability they need. The most common phrase a financial adviser will hear when speaking to people in retirement is 'I'm too old to tie my money up'. However, if you are to consider using the strategies already discussed in this book then you will see why it is beneficial to tie some money up so that you are getting the most out of it that you can.

Inflation

Inflation is the silent killer of retirement funds. If you are using the interest created by your funds as income, your capital is never growing and although that value always remains the same, it is being eroded by inflation everyday. You may think this does not matter so much when you first retire and you just want the security of knowing exactly what you have but when you get to a point where you need a lump sum, either for an emergency or long term care and your capital buys you half what you thought it would – it matters.

In retirement you have no way, other than working, to increase the value of your money. It is therefore vital that your money works as hard for you as it possibly can. By leaving it in savings accounts not earning any interest it is being eaten away by inflation everyday. This is the easiest way to end up with less than you started with even though it will still say the same amount on your statement.

Interest as income

Unless you have diligently saved into your cash ISA's every year you will be paying tax at your highest rate on the interest you receive from your savings. This can massively reduce what you get as a monthly income in retirement.

When interest rates were high, it was quite possible to live off the interest produced from cash. Advisers warned their clients against the risk of doing this but it seemed so unlikely that rates would fall, many didn't listen. With interest rates now being as low as they are all of the warnings have come to fruition.

When you can no longer live off the interest that is produced from your cash, what do you do? You start to use the capital to top it up. This is all well and good if you have a bottomless pit of money but if you don't, you begin a never ending downward spiral towards having nothing. As you spend the capital, the amount of interest that can be earned from it reduces and (even if interest rates increase), you will never have the same amount as you had before. In addition to this, the cost of living increases each year, resulting in you having to take an ever increasing amount from your capital until eventually you end up with nothing at all.

In addition to this risk, you also have to actively manage your finances to get the most out of them. Even if you choose not to follow the strategy outlined in this book and you stick to one bond that matures every year, you will still have to go through the process of reinvesting it every year and when you are in your nineties this is not a pleasant process.

Inheritance Tax and Long Term Care
As with property, you are not able to protect your money from Inheritance Tax or Long Term Care when it is kept in cash.

Investments

There are numerous advantages to using investments to create an income in retirement but firstly let's get the main disadvantage out of the way. Yes, if you invest you can end up getting back more, less or the same as what you originally invested (as with property). The value of the investment will fluctuate during the time that you hold it and there will be periods when it is worth less. However unlike cash but the same as property, the longer you hold it for the more chance there is that it will increase in value and keep pace with inflation, being worth more in the long run.

When making a comparison between investments and cash in retirement the best thing to do is consider one as being a rock and the other a sponge.

 If you are using your interest as an income then your cash is like a rock. It is a solid amount that does not change.

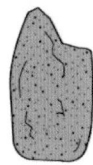 When you have to use some of your capital to enhance your income then you are chipping a bit off your rock.

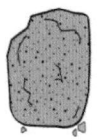 Because your rock is a solid mass it cannot grow and the more you chip away at it, the smaller it becomes!

 If you continually chip away at your capital, you can end up with nothing.

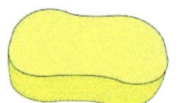 Investments are more like a sponge. You have the initial amount that you invest;

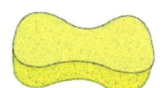 As the markets go down (or you need some of the capital), it shrivels up.

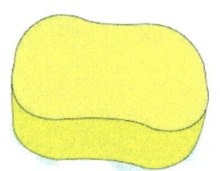 But just like water to a sponge, good news to the stock market (or growth) means that the sponge regains it shape and grows.

Time is often the main objection those who are retiring have to investing. 'I don't have time to let it run its course', or 'I don't want to tie my money up now that I am retired'. The question to consider here is - do you know when you are going to die? Is it going to be in two years' time? Or is it going to be in twenty years' time? With people living so much longer these days, when you retire at sixty there is a high chance that you are still going to be around in thirty years' time. Therefore how can you realistically say that you don't have time to invest or tie money up? In fact the longer you do survive the more important it is that some of your money is working that bit harder for you, as previously discussed. Just like the strategy outlined earlier, whether you need an income or not, some of your money needs to be for immediate use and some needs to be put away to grow.

Income
With investments you can choose whether you would like a planned income, so you know exactly what you will get each month regardless of interest rates or market fluctuations. Or you can have a natural income that has the potential to grow with inflation but is variable and can also go down.

Natural income
The income produced by gilts, corporate bonds and growth and income shares is known as a natural income because it is the income produced naturally by those investments.

If you are cautious and the fluctuating value of your capital causes you great stress then you could build an individual gilt and corporate bond ladder, as discussed on earlier in the book. The benefit of this is that you will know the income that is coming in and for how long it will do so. The downside is that, like cash your funds will not have a chance to grow in line with inflation. You also have the risk that if one of the companies folds then you could potentially lose the funds invested in it. For this reason you may prefer to invest in a pooled gilt and or corporate bond fund rather than individual holdings. By pooling such investments you change their natural behaviour and as an investment, they start acting more like shares. You will experience fluctuations in the capital value and you are not guaranteed to get back the amount you put in (as you are when they are individual holdings), the income that you receive can also go up and down. The diagram below explains how and why these changes occur.

Why <u>income</u> from a corporate bond fund fluctuates

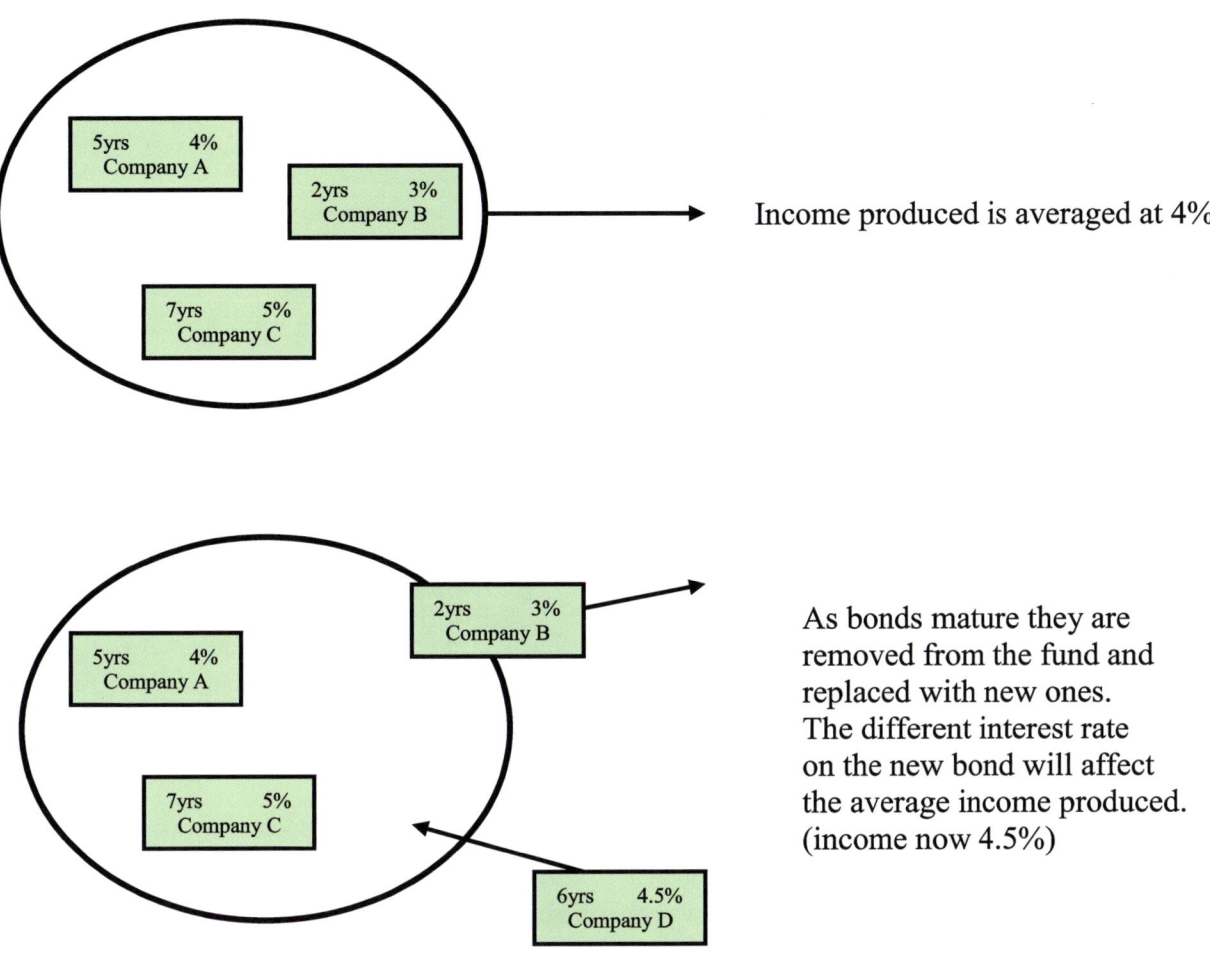

Why the <u>capital</u> value of a corporate bond fund fluctuates

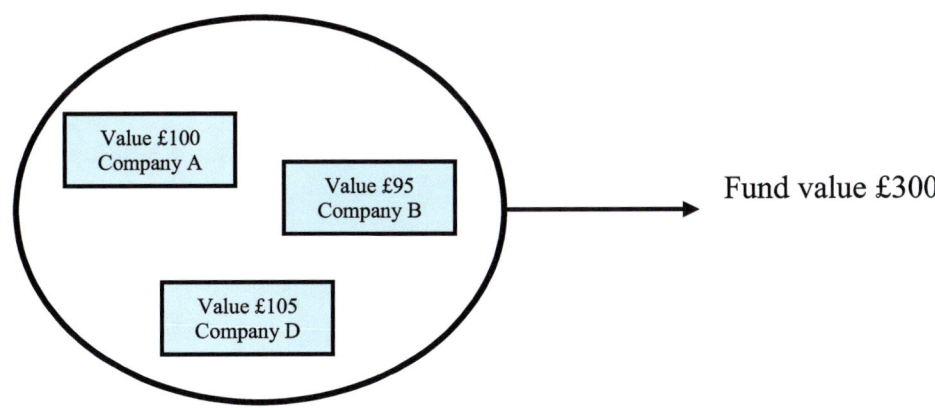

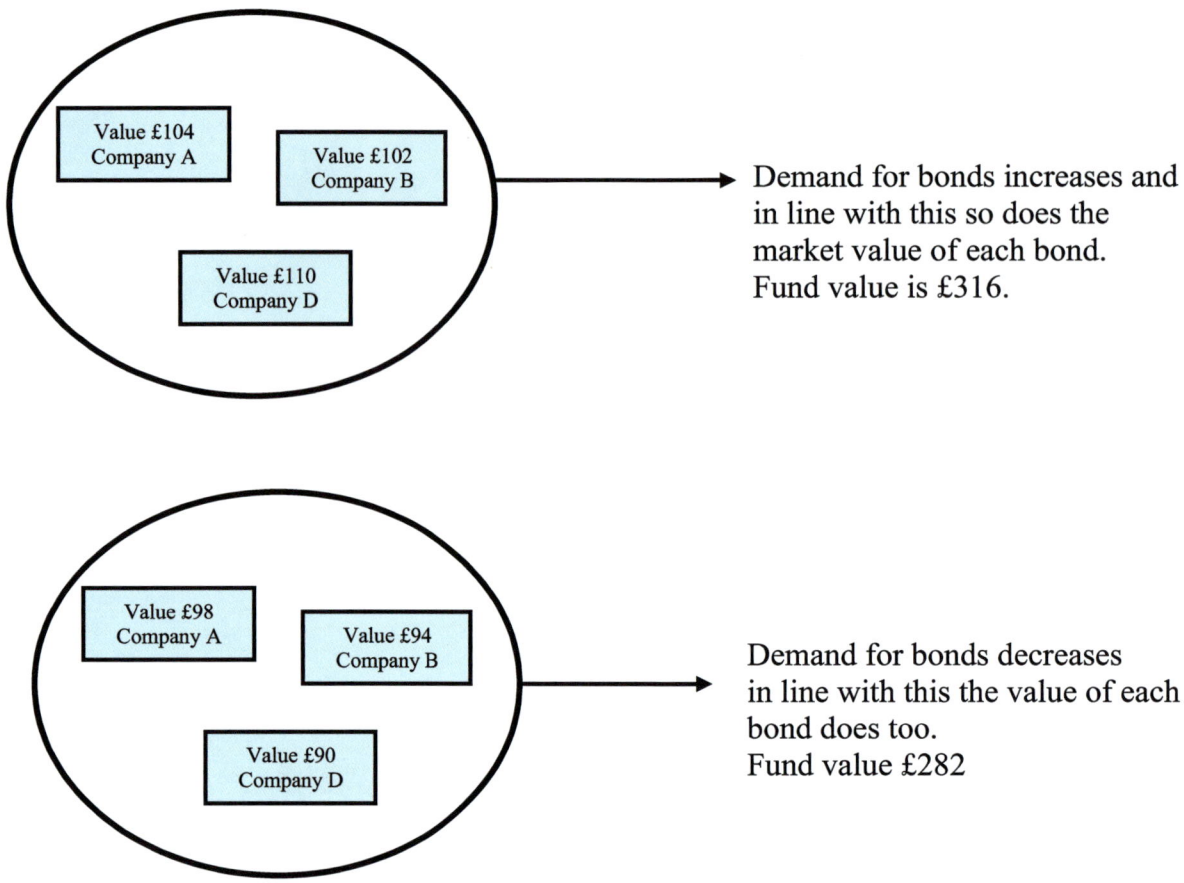

Demand for bonds increases and in line with this so does the market value of each bond. Fund value is £316.

Demand for bonds decreases in line with this the value of each bond does too. Fund value £282

Shares

The alternative investment for producing a natural income is growth and income shares, (middle lane of the motorway) where the dividend creates the income. If you were to do this by purchasing individual shares, then you need to ensure that the dividends paid out by each company are done so in different months or quarters, to give you a regular income (similar to a bond ladder). If however, you choose to use a pooled fund, then either a monthly or quarterly income can be provided to you.

This type of income usually pays well and it is very likely to grow in line with inflation as companies increase their dividend payments to attract more shareholders. However it must be noted that there will be times when a company may need to cancel/defer dividend payments and this will affect your income. For this reason it is recommended to use pooled investments instead of having an individual share portfolio as one company not paying its dividend is going to have a much smaller impact on your income.

This type of investment will see the capital value rise and fall. The key to managing this is remembering that whilst you are creating an income, unlike cash, you are also giving your capital the chance to grow in value over the longer term.

You can make both of these natural incomes' tax efficient by holding them in investment ISA's. If you have growth and income shares you will still pay the 10%

tax credit but nothing else, no matter what level of taxpayer you are. Not forgetting that you are also protecting your growth from Capital Gains Tax. If you have corporate bonds you will receive the full income produced by the bond.

Please note that it is possible to purchase pooled investments that contain both corporate bonds and growth and income shares, producing a diversified income, as well as the opportunity for a small amount of capital growth.

Planned income

If you would prefer to have a planned income so that you always know exactly what is coming in, then a capital investment bond can be used to provide this. Regardless of whether the investments inside the bond produce a natural income or not, the bond will produce an income of 5% annually, (calculated from the initial investment value). This income is regarded as being a return of your capital and is therefore not taxed.

Inheritance Tax Planning and Long Term Care

Capital investment bonds can be used as a strategy for both Inheritance Tax and Long Term Care planning. You must seek professional guidance in using these for such strategies.

Summary

- You have three choices to create an income in retirement; Property, Cash and Investments. Property will create you an income whilst giving your capital the chance to grow in the long term but it is not a liquid asset and will take time and money to realise any funds. You will have to pay Capital Gains Tax and Income Tax on any growth or income produced.

- Cash is very liquid but by creating an income from your interest, you are not allowing your capital any chance to grow and so it will be eroded by inflation over time. In addition to this, as you use the capital you have no way to replace it and you run the risk of eventually whittling it down to nothing. You will pay Income Tax on the interest if it is not inside an ISA.

- Investments can produce you different types of income according to your needs (variable or planned). There are different ways to make the Income Tax efficient and you can protect your growth from Capital Gains Tax. Although your capital value fluctuates, over the longer term you are producing an income whilst giving your capital the chance to grow. Certain investments can also be beneficial tools in creating a strategy to protect your families wealth from Inheritance Tax and Long Term Care costs.

- To conclude, the best thing to do with your finances in retirement is to continue with the larder, fridge and freezer concept and have a little bit in each.

Printed in Great Britain
by Amazon.co.uk, Ltd.,
Marston Gate.